SPORTS AND ATHLETICS PREPARATION,
PERFORMANCE, AND PSYCHOLOGY

MENTAL PRACTICE IN SPORT

TWENTY CASE STUDIES

SPORTS AND ATHLETICS PREPARATION, PERFORMANCE, AND PSYCHOLOGY

Additional books in this series can be found on Nova's website under the Series tab.

Additional E-books in this series can be found on Nova's website under the E-books tab.

SPORTS AND ATHLETICS PREPARATION, PERFORMANCE, AND PSYCHOLOGY

MENTAL PRACTICE IN SPORT

TWENTY CASE STUDIES

BORIS BLUMENSTEIN
AND
IRIS ORBACH

Nova Science Publishers, Inc.
New York

For permission to use material from this book please contact us:
Telephone 631-231-7269; Fax 631-231-8175
Web Site: http://www.novapublishers.com

NOTICE TO THE READER

The Publisher has taken reasonable care in the preparation of this book, but makes no expressed or implied warranty of any kind and assumes no responsibility for any errors or omissions. No liability is assumed for incidental or consequential damages in connection with or arising out of information contained in this book. The Publisher shall not be liable for any special, consequential, or exemplary damages resulting, in whole or in part, from the readers' use of, or reliance upon, this material. Any parts of this book based on government reports are so indicated and copyright is claimed for those parts to the extent applicable to compilations of such works.

Independent verification should be sought for any data, advice or recommendations contained in this book. In addition, no responsibility is assumed by the publisher for any injury and/or damage to persons or property arising from any methods, products, instructions, ideas or otherwise contained in this publication.

This publication is designed to provide accurate and authoritative information with regard to the subject matter covered herein. It is sold with the clear understanding that the Publisher is not engaged in rendering legal or any other professional services. If legal or any other expert assistance is required, the services of a competent person should be sought. FROM A DECLARATION OF PARTICIPANTS JOINTLY ADOPTED BY A COMMITTEE OF THE AMERICAN BAR ASSOCIATION AND A COMMITTEE OF PUBLISHERS.

Additional color graphics may be available in the e-book version of this book.

Library of Congress Cataloging-in-Publication Data

Mental practice in sport : twenty case studies / editors, Boris Blumenstein and Iris Orbach.
p. cm.
Includes index.
ISBN 978-1-62100-324-3 (softcover)
1. Sports--Psychological aspects--Case studies. I. Blumenstein, Boris. II. Orbach, Iris.
GV706.4.M457 2011
796.01--dc23
2011034212

Published by Nova Science Publishers, Inc. † New York

CONTENTS

PREFACE

This book is comprised of seven chapters which center upon Psychological Skills Training (PST) for various sports and athletes. The idea of writing this book has been on our mind for several years. Our past experience in working with sportsmen and sportswomen led us to realize the importance of psychological support for athletic performance enhancement. We would like to summarize our theoretical and practical knowledge and bring it to athletes to be used in their path to success. We the authors, Dr. Boris Blumenstein (BB) and Dr. Iris Orbach (IO) share a similar road to sport psychology consultancy, which started on the track. BB was a competitive sprinter, and IO was a competitive long jumper for a period of more than ten years. Through our experience as professional athletes we realized the critical impact psychological factors can have on athletic performance enhancement. Therefore, each of us decided to pursue a career as a sport psychology consultant, earning our Ph.D.'s in Sport Psychology. In regard to applied work, BB has consulted the leading elite athletes from the former Soviet Union teams, and since 1990 has served as the sport psychology consultant of the Israeli Olympic delegations during four Summer Olympic Games (1996, 2000, 2004, and 2008). IO presently works with top younger athletes from various individual and teams sports. Our experience in working with athletes was a defining factor for us, and spurred us to think about a new psychological approach to applied practice and numerous directions for research projects. We hope this book can serve as a theoretical and practical source for those interested in the mental side of sport performance – sport psychology consultants, graduate students, researchers in sport psychology, sport science professionals, coaches, and athletes.

This book consists of twenty case studies which greatly facilitate the translation of psychological theory into everyday practice. There are numerous examples involving famous elite athletes, including those competing in European, World Championships, and Olympic medalists. The real-life examples cut across individual and team sports from 13 disciplines. In addition, psychological work with athletes with disability and sport injuries, as well as with youth athletes, is discussed.

Chapter 1 focuses on the principles and foundations of our approach, and provides suggestions for the integration and implications of PST programs in the athletic training process. Chapter 2 is devoted to an analysis of PST in combat sports (judo, taekwondo, and fencing). The PST programs are based on the periodization principle last for long- or short-term periods, and are provided in a systematic/non-systematic manner. Chapter 3 is concerned with PST programs from individual sports such as rhythmic gymnastics, windsurfing, swimming, pole vault, and kayaking. Psychological programs are based on the periodization principle, focusing on both laboratory and training settings, and discuss the importance of full cooperation with the coaching staff. Chapter 4 describes PST programs for the team sports of soccer and basketball, at both the professional and youth levels. Psychological work is applied in individual and group settings, and the significant impact of full cooperation with the coaching staff, parents, and pedagogical staff in sport academia is emphasized. Chapter 5 is concerned with PST programs for youth athletes from tennis, table tennis, judo, and basketball. Special attention is given to the relationship between the sport psychology consultant, coach, and parents. Chapter 6 focuses on three case studies from judo, table tennis, and sailing 470 for athletes with disability or sport injuries. The major idea of PST programs is the modification and development of psychological interventions suitable to the athletes' disability and injuries. Finally, Chapter 7 presents seven main points which are the basis for our psychological intervention approach. We demonstrate that the implementation of these central points in the training process has a major positive impact on athletic performance enhancement.

Enjoy your reading!
BB and IO

Chapter 1

CONCEPTUAL FRAMEWORK

ABSTRACT

"Chapter 1: Conceptual Framework" includes the theoretical background for the book. The chapter focuses on two main objectives. The first part of the chapter discusses an historical overview of sport and exercise psychology and the principles of our psychological consultation approach. In the second part of Chapter 1 our psychological skills training program, which includes three sub-programs, is described. Each of our intervention programs is based on the periodization principle, and is described in detail including the norms and steps used. Throughout the book the psychological skills training programs are used in various combinations and with different sport types, including individual and team sports.

INTRODUCTION

In the last three decades there has been a significant increase in athletic psychological preparation, as an important part of the athletic process and as a critical factor for athletic success. The main objective of psychological preparation is to develop psychological skills in order to enhance an athlete's ability to achieve sport excellence. To accomplish their best performance, athletes can acquire those skills through psychological skills training (PST). PST has been defined as the systematic application of procedures, "a complex, multilayer integrative approach to developing mental skills in athletes" (Vealey, 2007, p. 292). In this chapter we will discuss our PST approach to achieving the best athletic performance. More specifically, the main purpose of this chapter is to understand the historical and professional background of the development of the authors' approach to practicing psychology with athletes from different sports. We will start by presenting a short historical overview of the development and status of elite sport and the services of sport psychology in our country.

HISTORICAL OVERVIEW

In 1948, when the State of Israel was established, the physical training department was placed under the framework of the Ministry of Education and Culture. In 1960, the department was replaced by the newly-created Sport and Physical Education Authority, whose task was to supervise both competitive sport and physical education (Lidor and Bar-Eli, 1998; Lidor and Blumenstein, 2009).

Throughout the more than 60 years of Israel's history, sport has become a popular activity among citizens, not only as a recreational activity but also as a competitive activity. In 1984, the Ministry of Education, Sport, and Culture and the Israeli Olympic Committee established the Elite Sport Department. The main objective of the department was to provide optimal preparation to the elite athletes participating in Olympic Games and World and European championships. Moreover, the Elite Sport Department provides professional support not only to the athletes but also to coaches, athletic trainers, sport physicians, and sport psychologists.

There are a number of problems within the elite sport in Israel. Due to the low number of high-level athletes, there is little variety among the competitors, and therefore the level of competition in practice and events is relatively low. In addition, the hot climate most of the year has an impact on quality training processes. To overcome these obstacles, athletes and coaches often travel abroad for training camps and competition purposes (Blumenstein, 2001).

The most popular sports in Israel are soccer, basketball, judo, sailing, rhythmic gymnastics, and tennis. The first Olympic medals Israeli athletes achieved were in Barcelona, 1992. By the end of the Olympic Games in 2008 in Beijing, Israel had won five more Olympic medals – in judo, canoeing and windsurfing. Moreover, a grandmaster achievement is the holder of the 2009 Chess World Cup. . In Table 1.1 the Olympic medals and finals of the Israeli athletes are shown. In addition, there have been other notable achievements in European and World championships, mainly in judo, taekwondo, sailing, windsurfing, rhythmic gymnastics, and track and field.

These athletes' achievements have also influenced the development of sport sciences in Israel. More and more athletes, coaches, sport administrators, and sport policy makers have become aware of the contribution of sport sciences, such as sport medicine, biomechanics, sport nutrition, exercise physiology, and sport and exercise psychology, to sport performance enhancement (Lidor and Blumenstein, 2009). In this book our main focus will be on the athletes' mental preparation, from different skill levels and disciplines, emphasizing applications based on research findings.

Table 1.1. Olympic Medals of Israeli Athletes

	No. of Athletes	Gender M/F	No. Of Sport Discip.	Gold Medal	Silver Medal	Bronze Medal	Finals
Barcelona, 1992	30	25/5	10	–	Yael Arad, Judo	Oren Smadja, Judo	5 finals: Pole vault; Mistral; Sailing 470; Weight Lifting (2)
Atlanta, 1996	25	18/7	10	–	–	Gal Fridman, Windsurfing	3 finals: Judo, Swimming 4X100; Wrestling
Sydney, 2000	39	29/10	9	–	–	Michael Kalganov, Canoe/ Kayak K-500	8 finals: High junp; Pole vault; K-1000; Sailing (2) Mistral, 470; Swimming Wrestling
Athens, 2004	36	21/15	13	Gal Fridman, Windsurfing	–	Arik Zeevi, Judo	3 finals: Pole vault; K-500 (2)
Beijing, 2008	43	23/20	12	–	–	Shahar Zubari, Windsurfing	6 finals: Judo, Gymnastics (3); Sailing (2)

Background of Sport and Exercise Psychology

The roots of sport and exercise psychology in Israel were initiated by numerous research projects, conducted mainly in the Ribstein Center for Sport Medicine Sciences and Research and the Zinman College, both at the Wingate Institute. The main focuses of the research studies have been: the development of the Wingate 5-Step Approach (Blumenstein and Bar-Eli, 2005; Blumenstein, Bar-Eli, and Collins, 2002; Blumenstein, Bar-Eli, and Tenenbaum, 1997); learning strategies in motor skill acquisitions (Lidor and Singer, 2005); decision making in sport (Tenenbaum and Bar-Eli, 1993); rationality in sport (Bar-Eli, Lurie, and Breivik, 1999), and the effectiveness of various interventional mental programs on athletes performance (Blumenstein, Lidor, 2004; Blumenstein, Lidor, and Tenenbaum, 2005; Lidor, Blumenstein, and Tenenbaum, 2007, 2009). Many of these interventions have been developed by sport psychology consultants from the Elite Sport Department, which is supported both ideologically and financially by the Israeli Olympic Committee. In essence, sport psychologists are assigned to work with elite athletes, and are part of the professional staff that prepares the athletes for upcoming sporting events. This means that the sport psychologists attend practice sessions, team meetings and competitions. For example, in the last four summer Olympic Games the first author (BB) was an official member of the Israeli Delegation in the Olympic Village.

Principles and Foundations of Our Psychological Consultation Approach

Most athletes, coaches, and applied sport psychologists/consultations agree that psychological preparation (i.e., Psychological Skill Training; PST) is a vital determinant of athletic success (Hung, Lidor and Hackfort, 2009; Vealey, 2007).

During PST we teach/train our clients/athletes a number of mental practice skills that are intended to enhance the mental and emotional aspects of performance (Henschen, 2005; Vealey, 2007). Among these skills are attention and concentration (Moran, 2005, 2010), relaxation (Henschen, 2005), imagery (Morris, 2010), self-regulation of arousal (Weinberg, 2010; Williams and Krane, 2001), and self-confidence (Vealey, 2007), as well as cohesion and leadership for athletes participating in team sports (Vealey, 2007).

PST can include either a mental skill technique which can be used by itself or is part of a mental intervention package (Blumenstein and Weinstein, 2010; Vealey, 2007). The traditional mental skills techniques/strategies for PST are: relaxation/arousal regulation, imagery, goal setting, thought management, self-talk, biofeedback training, and pre-competition mental routines (Blumenstein and Weinstein, 2010; Henschen, 2005; Lidor, 2010; Moran, 2010; Vealey, 2007; Gould, 2001). These techniques are those most widely used by sport psychological consultants (Blumenstein and Weinstein, 2010; Vealey, 2007; Henchen, 2005; Gould, 2002) and have shown significant positive effects on athletic performance in numerous research studies (Vealey, 2007; Weinberg and Comar, 1994).

After years of reading other professional philosophies and accumulating practical experience, a sport psychologist can formulate his/her own personal philosophies to govern his/her psychological consulting style. After about 40 years in the sport psychology discipline (the first author), we will attempt to present our educational approach for PST (Figure 1.1). Its main objective is to teach the athlete psychological strategies/techniques for improving psychological skills relevant to sport discipline. This should lead to a positive effect on the athlete's personal development and performance. Several unique parameters of our PST approach follow:

1. PST is an integral part of the general athletic preparation, and is linked with other preparations, such as the physical, technical, and tactical.
2. Psychological skills can be developed in ways similar to physical skills.
3. PST is provided systematically and throughout a long-term period.
4. The PST program includes periodization and planning for each sport discipline.
5. The sport psychologist who teaches PST should be one of the professional staff, working on a regular basis with the individual athlete or the team.
6. The success of the PST depends on full cooperation between the sport psychology consultant and the coaching staff and athletes.

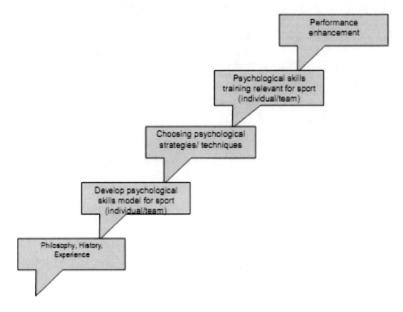

Figure 1.1. Schematic description of our PST approach.

In Figure 1.1, the parameters of our PST approach are presented. The case studies presented in this book are based on this framework.

PSYCHOLOGICAL SKILLS TRAINING PROGRAM

Our psychological program was composed of three sub-programs: the *Wingate 5-Step Approach* (W5SA; Blumenstein et al., 1997; Blumenstein and Bar-Eli, 2005; Blumenstein et al., 2002), the *Reaction/Response Training Program* (RTP: Blumenstein et al., 2005; Blumenstein and Weinstein, 2010), and the *Specific Psychological Training Program* (SPTP: Blumenstein and Lidor, 2007, 2008).

The Wingate 5-Step Approach: The *W5SA* is a self-regulation technique incorporating biofeedback (BFB) training. This technique enables athletes to transfer the psycho-regulative skills performed in sterile laboratory settings to real practice and competition settings, utilizing testing and various simulative materials (Blumenstein and Bar-Eli, 2005). The W5SA is composed of five stages: (a) *Introduction* (learning various self-regulation techniques, e.g., imagery, focusing-attention, and self-talk), (b) *Identification* (identifying and strengthening the most efficient BFB response modality), (c) *Simulation* (BFB training with simulated competitive stress), (d) *Transformation* (bringing mental preparation from the laboratory to the field), and (e) *Realization* (achieving optimal regulation in competition). Between each step a Self-Regulation Test (SRT) is conducted. The SRT is used to examine the athlete's baseline self-regulation level before the mental training program is applied, and later between each step of the program. A tentative concept of each step is presented below.

Self-Regulation Test: SRT is used to examine the athlete's baseline self-regulation level before the mental training program is applied, and later during the various steps of the program (Blumenstein et al., 1997; Blumenstein, et al., 2002). The SRT consists of four elements: rest, tension, relaxation, and competition. These were derived and modified from the autogenic training technique suggested by Schultz (1932). After recording the athlete's psychophysiological baseline (Heart Rate – HR, Electromyography – EMG, and Galvanic Skin Response – GSR), the athlete is asked to imagine him/herself in a laboratory setting, in resting, tense, relaxation, and competitive states, consecutively. Towards the end of each of these imagery phases, each lasting about 2 min, the athlete's psychophysiological responses (HR, EMG, and GSR) are recorded, to indicate the type of alteration in each response modality as well as its relative intensity. It should be noted that for diagnostic purposes, the changes recorded following the phase of competition imagery are of particular significance. The arrows in Table 1.2 represent the expected direction of positive change on each psychophysiological modality in each phase, when imagery is indeed effective (+).

According to our experience in HR and GSR modalities, the athlete received a + when a change of 10% in his/her responses was observed; in the EMG modality a + was received when a change of 20% was observed (Blumenstein and Orbach, 2011, in press). In SRT the athlete can achieve a maximum of 12 +, while a + represents a relevant changes according to Table

**Table 1.2. Direction of Psychophysiological Changes
from Baseline in SRT**

Physiological Responses	Four Imagery States			
	Rest	Tension	Relaxation	Competition
HR	↓	↑	↓	↑
EMG	↓	↑	↓	↑
GSR	↑	↓	↑	↓

Table 1.3. SRT before the Preparation Phase

	Base*	Rest		+/-	Tension		+/-	Relaxation		+/-	Competition		+/-
		B*	A*		B	A		B	A		B	A	
HR bpm	68	70	64	+	72	74	-	72	66	+	68	76	+
EMG μV	2.2-2.4	2.4	1.8	+	2.6	2.8	-	2.7	2.0	+	2.6	3.7	+
GSR kΩ	650-670	664	696	-	678	650	-	680	646	-	660	620	-

B* = Before; A* = After; Base* = Baseline

2 in HR, EMG, and GSR channels in the four imagery states. After more than 10 years of applying our program in different sports, we can conclude that our elite athletes achieved the following in SRT:

- High self-regulation level: 11-12 +.
- Average self-regulation level: 8-10 +.
- Low self-regulation level: 6-7 +.

An example of SRT before the preparation phase of a 17 year-old experienced swimmer is presented in Table 1.3.

Usually, young athletes achieve 4-6 + in the first SRT in the beginning of the W5SA process (non-athletes achieve 2-3+). As can be seen in Table 3, the athlete achieved a 6 +. This result is considered as a low self-regulation level based on our norms. From this point the athlete is ready to start the process of the W5SA. The following numbers represent the direction we recommend should be achieved in each step. It is important to consider parameters such as personality and sport type, which can have an effect on the numbers and session contents.

Introduction: The first step takes place in a laboratory setting, where the athlete is introduced to the various pieces of psychophysiological equipment, including the computerized BFB and TV + Video Camera Recorder (VCR) equipment. This step, about 10-15 sessions, 2-3 times a week, with each session lasting about 55-60 min, consists of teaching the athlete to regulate his or her mental state through observing the psychophysiological responses on the screen. The athlete begins with the frontalis EMG feedback, with surface electrodes placed on the frontalis muscle in accordance with Kondo, Canter, and Bean (1977). Later in this step (and in all the following steps), the athlete also uses other biofeedback modalities, such as HR, breathing, and GSR.

The main goal of the introductory step is to achieve a stable process in which the athlete is relaxed for about 2-3 min, maintains a deep relaxation for about 5-10 min, and then rehearses excitation for about 2-3 min (Blumenstein et al., 2002; Blumenstein, Tenenbaum, Bar-Eli, and Pie, 1995). After terminating the introductory phase, the athlete undergoes a second SRT to indicate his/her psychoregulative level and to observe the specific modalities pertaining to his/her individual responses.

Step 1: Introduction	
Session #	Content of Session
1	SRT, learning muscle relaxation
2-3	Muscle relaxation: 3-5 min x 2-3 times
	Concentration exercise: 1 min x 5-7 times
4	Muscle relaxation: 3-5 min x 2-3 times
	Imagery (nature scenes): 3-5 min x 2-3 times
	Learning EMG BFB (audio-visual versions)
5	Muscle relaxation + Imagery: 3-5 min x 2-3 times
	Learning EMG BFB, HR BFB (audio-visual versions)
6	Relaxation + Imagery using EMG BFB: 3-5 min x 2-3 times
	Learning GSR BFB (audio-visual versions)
7	BFB games [*] levels 9-10 with GSR BFB with relaxation music background
8	Relaxation – excitation waves with GSR BFB: 1 min x 8-10 times
	Concentration exercises with GSR: 10-20 sec x 10-15 times
9	Relaxation – excitation waves with EMG/HR: 1 min x 8-10 times
	Concentration exercises with GSR: 10-20 sec x 10-15 times
10	Relaxation – excitation waves with GSR BFB: 1 min x 8-10 times
	Concentration exercises with GSR: 10-20 sec x 10-15 times
11	Second SRT, BFB games levels 9-10 with GSR BFB

[*] see Figures 1.1 and 1.2

BFB games consist of a variety of relaxation games with GSR BFB, such as the fish game by ProRelax equipment (Mind Life Solutions, Ltd.) (see Figures 1.2 and 1.3).

Figure 1.2. A picture from the "Fish" game.

The BFB training took place in a sport psychology laboratory, with a Mindlife biofeedback device (i.e., ProRelax by Mindlife Solutions, Ltd.) that monitors skin conductance via two 5-mm-diameter electrodes connected with velcro bands. The electrodes are connected to a sensor box and the raw data is transmitted via infra red (IR) connection to the receiver box (Blumenstein and Orbach, 2011, in press).

An example of a game by the ProRelax program is the "fish" game. In this dynamic game the athlete uses relaxation and concentration skills to move the fish forward from the left to the right side and to transform the picture to other forms, such as to a mermaid and finally to a woman . In addition, the sensitivity of the game can be changed from 1 to 10 (i.e., difficult-easy). The "fish" game is accompanied by special relaxation music. Usually, the best elite athletes performed this game for 1:30-1:45 seconds with sensitivity 5. The same animated principle is used in other BFB games of the ProRelax program, using themes such as "flight", "history", and "nature".

Figure 1.3. A picture from the "Fish" game (continued).

Identification: In the second step (which included about 15 sessions) the goal is to identify and strengthen the athlete's most efficient response modality on the BFB. This modality is modified by the individual's specific personal psychophysiologic characteristics, and by the characteristics of the sport discipline in which the athlete competes. Moreover, different sports require different response modalities (Blumenstein et al., 2002). For example, in judo or wrestling, in which performance involves high levels of tactile and proprioceptive sensitivity and intense emotional involvement, EMG and GSR seem to be the most efficient modalities to measure. In contrast, rifle shooting demands a shooter's postural' breathing, and muscle stability, and therefore EEG is more suitable (Landers et al., 1991). Finally, HR and breathing frequency measurements are more useful for long-distance running or swimming, which require mainly cardiopulmonary and cardiomuscular endurance (Blumenstein et al., 2002).

In this step, the athlete must be able to perform, in the laboratory setting, the required relaxation-excitation cycle quickly, accurately, and reliably. The average numbers for an elite athlete are as follows: To achieve EMG relaxation, the athlete's data should be within the limits 0.8-1.0 µV during 1-3 min or excitation with imagery within the limits 2.2-2.6 µV during 1-3 min. In addition, to achieve GSR relaxation, the athlete's data should be Δ150-190 kΩ during 1-3 min, or excitation with imagery, in which the athlete's data should be Δ 200-250 kΩ during 1-3 min.

Step 2: Identification	
Session #	Content of Session *
1	Muscle relaxation with GSR BFB: 3 min x 5 times, Δ20-30 kΩ Concentration exercise with GSR BFB: 20-30 sec x 10 times, Δ10-20 kΩ
2	Muscle relaxation with EMG BFB: 3-5 min x 5 times, from baseline ↓ 1.6-1.4 µV Concentration exercise with GSR BFB: 20-30 sec x 10 times, Δ10-20 kΩ
3	Muscle relaxation with HR BFB: 3-5 min x 5 times, from baseline ↓ of 10% Concentration exercise with GSR BFB: 20-30 sec x 10 times, Δ10-20 kΩ
4-5	Excitation with EMG/GSR BFB + imagery (competition scene): 1-2 min x 5-7 times Concentration exercise with GSR BFB: 10-20 sec x 10 times, Δ10-20 kΩ
6	Excitation with HR BFB + imagery (competition scene): 1-2 min x 5-7 times Concentration exercise with GSR BFB: 10-20 sec x 10 times, Δ10-20 kΩ
7-8	Relaxation (R)–Excitation (E) waves with EMG/GSR BFB + imagery (nature/ competition scene): R 3 min-E 2 min x 5 times Concentration exercise with GSR BFB: 10 sec x 10 times, Δ10-20 kΩ
9-10	Relaxation (R)–Excitation (E) waves with HR/GSR BFB + imagery (nature/ competition scene): R 3 min-E 2 min x 5 times Concentration exercise with GSR BFB: 10 sec x 10 times, Δ10-20 kΩ
11	BFB games with GSR, levels 7-8 Muscle relaxation with GSR BFB and music: 15-20 min
12	Third SRT, Biofeedback games levels 7-8 with GSR BFB

* This example is more relevant for combat sport, in which EMG/GSR BFB are the dominant modalities.

Simulation: In the third step (which included 10-15 sessions) the athlete performs the learned skills (i.e., relaxation, concentration, and excitation abilities) with different simulated competitive stress. The athlete is exposed to the following situations:

- "Positive" motivation statements (M+) are provided, such as "wonderful", "today is your day", "you are looking good", and "you can do it".
- "Negative" motivation statements (M-) are provided, such as "you are playing very badly", "it is not your day", "what are you doing?", and "the referee is against you".
- Video scenes from competitive situations in which the athlete competed are presented on the VCR screen. While watching the scenes, a mental cycle of relaxation-excitation states is rehearsed. These states are geared to the particular competition needs at each moment of competition, as well as the athlete's personal characteristics. For example, in taekwondo and boxing there are several breaks between the rounds and in fencing and judo there are breaks only between the matches. During these breaks, it is advisable for the athlete to be engaged in some self-regulatory activity that is focused mainly on the transition from relaxation to excitation, in order to "psych up" for the next round. In contrast, following an entire match, a transition from excitation to relaxation is needed. This enables the athlete to learn his/her moves and prepare for the next match. This activity may last for 1-5 min, depending on the athlete's specific requirements. To optimally use the available options, the sport psychologist should acquire extensive knowledge about both the athlete and the particular sport (Blumenstein et al., 2002).

The athlete practices the shifts from one mental state to another by observing 5-10 scenes, lasting for about 10-30 sec each. The order of the scenes may be of importance, depending, among other things, on the athlete's preferences. VCR apparatus is used to simulate competitive stress presented to the athlete. The main principle guiding the use of VCR in this step is a gradual elevation of the simulated stress.

At the end of the third step the athlete is re-tested using the SRT procedure. However, in contrast to the previous steps, the SRT procedure is now accompanied by VCR presentations (Blumenstein et al., 2002).

Step 3: Simulation	
Session #	Content of Session
1	Muscle relaxation with HR BFB and M+/M-: 1-3 min x 5 times, ↓ 10% Concentration exercise with GSR BFB and M+/M-: 20-30 sec x 5 times, Δ10-20 kΩ
2	Muscle relaxation with EMG BFB and M+/M-: 1-3 min x 5 times, from baseline ↓ 1.6-1.4 μV Concentration exercise with GSR BFB and M+/M-: 20-30 sec x 5 times, Δ10-20 kΩ
3	Muscle relaxation with GSR BFB and M+/M-: 1-3 min x 5 times, from baseline ↓ of 10% Concentration exercise with GSR BFB and M+/M-: 20-30 sec x 5 times, Δ10-20 kΩ
4-5	Relaxation with EMG/GSR BFB + VCR (competition scenes): 1-3 min x 5 times Concentration exercise with GSR BFB: 10-20 sec x 5 times, Δ10-20 kΩ
6	Excitation with HR BFB and M+/M-: 1-2 min x 5 times, ↑ 10% Concentration exercise with GSR BFB: 10-20 sec x 5 times, Δ10-20 kΩ
7	Excitation with EMG/GSR BFB and M+/M-: 1-2 min x 5 times Concentration exercise with GSR BFB: 10-20 sec x 5 times, Δ10-20 kΩ
8-9	Excitation with EMG/GSR BFB and VCR (competition scene): 1-2 min x 5 times Concentration exercise with GSR BFB: 10-20 sec x 5 times, Δ10-20 kΩ
10-13	Relaxation–Excitation waves with EMG/GSR BFB and VCR using nature and competition scenes: (Relaxation 3 min-Excitation 2 min) x 5 times Concentration exercise with GSR BFB: 10 sec x 10 times, Δ10-20 kΩ
14	BFB games with GSR, levels 7-8 Muscle relaxation with GSR BFB and music: 15-20 min
15	Fourth SRT, BFB games levels 7-8 with GSR BFB

Transformation: In the fourth step (which includes approximately 10 sessions), the athlete mentally prepares for a specific upcoming competition. The material learned and rehearsed by the athlete in steps 1-3 is transferred to actual training settings while using portable BFB devices, in contrast to the laboratory setting in which the previous steps were conducted. The settings can come in different forms, depending on the sport.

Step 4: Transformation	
Session #	Content of Session
1-5	Using portable EMG/GSR BFB in different locations, such as a bus, hotel room, etc., and different training situations, such as before/after warm-ups, races, games, matches, etc.
6-10	Using portable EMG/GSR BFB for improving pre-competitive routine, concentration, and athlete's competition behavior.
11	Fifth SRT with VCR.

Thus, the main purpose of this step is to enable the athlete to enter real future competitions with improved self-regulation abilities.

Realization: In the fifth step the athlete applies the previously-acquired mental techniques during competition. Essentially, the application is very similar to that practiced in the previous step, but at this stage it is applied during the competition itself. The athlete begins by applying the procedure in relatively 3-5 less important competitions until the athlete is ready for more important competitions. This ensures that the athlete gradually learns to cope with increasingly difficult situations and to become less crisis-vulnerable. The final SRT is conducted in a laboratory setting.

REACTION TRAINING PROGRAM (RTP)

The main objective of the RTP is to enhance the athletes' responses under real-life settings (e.g., combat sport contests). The program consists of several reaction-time (RT) tasks, such as simple RT (1 stimulus, 1 response); two choice RT (2 stimuli, 2 response); and discrimination RT (2 stimuli, 1 response). A computer simulation is used, and several factors are adopted during training in order to expose the athlete to more real-life competitive situations. Among these factors are a video demonstration of actual combats, external distractions such as noise, and competitions between two athletes (e.g., judokas) performing the reaction-time tasks at the same time (Blumenstein et al., 2005). General descriptions, sets of training, and procedure of RTP are discussed in detail elsewhere (Blumenstein et al., 2005; Blumenstein and Weinstein, 2010).

Following are accumulated data, levels and demands that are required when applying RTP. Several *stress factors* accompanied RTP. The response tasks are performed under the following situations (Blumenstein and Weinstein, 2010):

(a) Ordinary laboratory settings
(b) Positive and negative verbal motivation (M+/M-)
(c) Performance under precise demands
(d) Reward/punishment for performance
(e) Performance under "true" competition noise (competition audio clips)
(f) Performance under "true" competition sights (competition video clips)
(g) Combination of situations a-f.

The first author's extensive research and applied experience from 1992 up to the present has included working with top Israeli athletes, both males and females, from the following combat sports: judo (N = 23), taekwondo (N = 10), fencing (N = 6), wrestling (N = 5), and boxing (N = 2). In this period they achieved one bronze Olympic medal, one gold and two silver medals from World championships, and 13 medals from European championships (7 gold, 4 silver, 2 bronze). In addition, these athletes achieved two gold medals from youth world championships and two silver medals from the Universiada . From our extensive work with athletes we realized that in RTP special attention needs to be given to the ratio between "fast" and "slow" RT, beyond the importance of time reaction. To exemplify this point, based on the numerous mental sessions working with RTP, we found that the time limit for "fast" RT was < 200msec and for "slow" RT > 200ms. This balance point can serve as a good indicator of a performance goal and can characterize performance quality. For example, a process was initiated with a 2-3/12-13 ratio (2-3 fast and 12-13 slow RT); following 1-2 months of training, the athlete achieved an 8/7 ratio (8 fast and 7 slow RT) or 10/5 ratio; right before the competition a 14/1 ratio or even 15/0 was recorded. We found three quality levels for combat sports, as can be seen in Table 1.4.

Table 1.4. Quality Levels for RTP in Combat Sports

Levels	Initial Level for Combat Sport (scores before training)		
	15 Simple RT: M=200-220ms; SD=±40-50; ratio 3-6/12-9	30 Choice RT: M=240-265ms; SD=±40-50; ratio 2-3/13-12	30 Discrimination RT: M=210-230ms; SD=±40-50; ratio 1-2/14-13
Level 1	175-185 ms; ±30-35 ratio 8-9/7-6	200-210 ms; ±30-35 ratio 8-9/7-6	185-195 ms; ±30-35 ratio 8-9/7-6
Level 2	155-165 ms; ±20-25 ratio 11-12/4-3	175-185 ms; ±20-25 ratio 10-11/5-4	165-175 ms; ±20-25 ratio 11-12/4-3
Level 3	135-145 ms; ±10-15 ratio 14-15/1-0	155-165 ms; ±10-15 ratio 13-14/2-1	145-155 ms; ±10-15 ratio 13-14/2-1

Table 1.5. Best Results Achieved by Elite Combat Athletes before Successful Competitions

Sports	Simple RT	Choice RT	Discrimination RT
Judo	107 ms±15-20 ratio 15/0	136 ms±20-25 ratio 14/1	117 ms±15-20 ratio 15/0
Taekwondo	110 ms±20-25 ratio 14/1	126 ms±15-20 ratio 13/2	122 ms±20-25 ratio 14/1
Fencing	105 ms±25-30 ratio 13/2	117 ms±20-25 ratio 13/2	97 ms±25-30 ratio 14/1

Table 1.5 shows the best results achieved by elite combat athletes before important and successful competitions.

Specific Psychological Training Program (SPTP) is composed of mental skill techniques such as focusing attention, imagery, self-talk, goal-setting and relaxation, which were developed by the sport psychology consultant throughout many years of professional practice. These techniques have also been used by other sport psychology consultants who work with athletes at the elite level (Henschen, 2005; Moran, 2005). When performing these techniques, the current physical and psychological state of the athlete, as well as the specific preparation phase and periodization of the training program, were taken into account (Blumenstein and Weinstein, 2010; Holliday, Burton, Sun, Hammermeister, Naylor, and Friegang,., 2008; Balague, 2000). SPTS includes three phases: the Learning, Modified, and Applied phases. In the *Learning* phase athletes acquire fundamental psychological techniques in a laboratory setting, namely in controlled and sterile conditions, in order to enable the athletes to acquire the basic foundations of each strategy. In the *Modified* phase, after progress is made in the laboratory setting, psychological skills are adapted in line with technical-tactical purposes and the sports' requirements . Finally, in the *Applied* phase psychological techniques are part of the preperformance and precompetitive routine, and are applied in actual practice sessions and competitions where the athletes are exposed to more authentic situations and real-life distracters (Table 1.5). For example, initially muscle relaxation techniques are taught and practiced for long periods of time (e.g., intervals of 5 to 10 min) within a laboratory setting, in a quiet and distraction-free environment. Then, relaxation is performed with stress factors (noises, comments, films) for short periods of time (e.g., intervals of 1 to 3 min). Eventually, relaxation becomes more sport-specific and helps the athletes cope with the specific technical-tactical demands of the training program and competition (e.g., rapid relaxation before matches and games, and between attempts). The same logic and sequence is provided for other psychological techniques, such as imagery and attention-focusing strategies, self-talk, and goal setting. The SPTS is usually provided as an independent program or as part of an intervention package which is applied in preparation and competition phases before important events. The techniques being used as part of the SPTP are adjusted based on the demands of the sport (i.e., individual and team), the periodization of the specific sport, and the needs of the athletes and the coaches (Blumenstein and Lidor, 2007; Blumenstein, Lidor, and Tenenbaum, 2008; Lidor et al., 2007).

PERIODIZATION OF PST INTERVENTIONS

It has been reported that the majority of mental training techniques are used during competitions, not during training (Frey, Laguna, and Ravizza, 2003). This may be related to the reality that effective mental training processes cannot stand alone, and should be integrated with and be parallel to additional elements of athletic preparation, such as the physical, technical, and tactical elements, and also within the training periodization phases (Balague, 2000; Blumenstein et al., 2005; Carrera and Bompa, 2007; Holliday et al., 2008). According to the theory and methodology of sport training, a basic and fundamental principle of athlete preparation is training periodization (Bompa, 1999; Carrera and Bompa, 2007; Zatsiorsky, 1995). Periodization is a planning tool for developing the athlete's training program (Smith, 2003). Basically, the periodization has three major phases: Preparatory (general and specific), competitive, and transitory. Each phase is comprised of four fundamental preparations: Physical, technical, tactical, and psychological. Periodization utilizes long-term planning to construct the training process into specific time periods (cycles): long- (macrocycle), medium- (mesocycle), and short-term (microcycle) cycles. The long cycle can last between a few months to a year; the medium cycle can last between a few weeks to a month, and the short cycle can last up to a week (Issurin, 2007). When applying our psychological program, our main focus is on the incorporation of the mental session with the athlete's training program, and linking it with the other preparations: physical, technical, tactical. Moreover, we modify the mental sessions based on the volume and intensity of the athlete's physical training. For example, a large number of exercises and repetitions with low intensity are given to the athlete during the *Preparation* phase of the physical training. The Preparation phase includes general (GP) and specific (SP) parts. The main objective of the GP phase is to improve the athlete's working capacity, strength, and endurance. Therefore, during the mental session the athlete works on relaxation for recovery purposes, motivation, goal setting techniques, the first two steps of the W5SA (i.e., Introduction and part of Identification), and the first level of the RTP. The main objective of the SP phase is to further develop the athlete's physical ability according to the unique physical and physiological characteristics of the sport (Bompa, 1999; Carrera and Bompa, 2007). For example, combat sport demands that the athlete execute a variety of technical elements while practicing with different opponents (Pedro and Durbin, 2001). Therefore, during the mental session the focus is on concentration and imagery techniques, in which the athlete visualizes technical elements of him/herself and his/her opponents. Moreover, the Identification and the Simulation steps of the W5SA and the second level of RTP are practiced (see Figure 1.4).

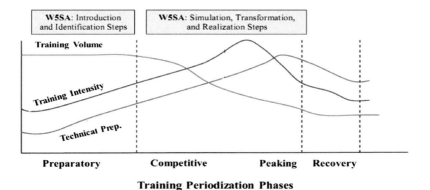

Figure 1.4. Periodization of the W5SA.

Table 1.6. Periodization of PST Programs

	TRAINING PHASES			
	Preparation		Competition	Recovery
	General	Specific		
Setting	Lab	Lab-Training	Lab-Training-Competition	Lab
Using stress distracters	a, b	c, d	e, f, g	-
Psychological sub-programs and techniques:				
RTP	**First level**	**Second level**	**Third level**	
SPTP:	**Learning Phase**	**Modified Phase**	**Applied Phase**	
Relaxation	Muscle relaxation (long)	Relaxation in practice (short)	Relaxation in pre-competitive routine (rapid)	Relaxation for recovery
Imagery	From external to internal imagery	Internal imagery of technical-tactical aspects of performance	Imagery is part of preperformance and precompetitive routine. Imagery of performance (key technical elements)	
Self-talk	Before and during training	Stopping negative thoughts in practice	Key words, stopping negative thoughts in competition	
Concentration	Variety of concentration exercises	Fast and intensive concentration in practice	Concentration in pre-competition routine and performance	
Goal setting	Training goal and plan	Technical and tactical goals, positive attitude goals	Performance goals	Long-term goals
W5SA	Introduction, Identification	Identification, Simulation	Transformation, Realization	

In the *Competition* phase, the intensity of the performed technical elements increases and the repetitions decrease, while the total time of training decreases. A variety of real environmental factors related to the specific sport are taken into account. In addition, the tactical preparation of the athlete is a significant factor in this phase.

Taking the above into account, during mental training sessions the athlete practices concentration and imagery techniques with competitive stress (e.g., use of recorded competitive films and noises), arousal regulation with different stress distractions, the last three steps of the W5SA, and the third level of the RTP. To strengthen the link between the mental sessions and performance during competition, beyond imagery clarity, we require that the athlete duplicate the imagery time to the actual competition time (judoka images for 5 minutes a match which lasts 5 min in competition; imagery for individual rhythmic gym lasts for about 1:30, etc.). In the *Transition* phase mental recovery, such as relaxation, listening to music, and breathing exercise, is used, incorporating BFB devices. Our approach is summarized in Table 1.6.

CONCLUSION

To summarize, the following points relate to the intervention programs discussed in this chapter:

1. Planned and integrated as part of the general preparation program of the athlete, linked with his/her basic physical, technical, and tactical preparations.

2. Require systematical mental practice sessions similarly to the physical training.

3. Periodization of PST programs has the potential framework for enhancing the effectiveness of psychological preparation and athletic performance.

4. An athlete who had experience with one of our intervention programs can start the mental preparation in the next training season, from different stages. For example, in the W5SP there is no need to start from the Introduction step each season. Usually an athlete with experience in this intervention program can continue from the Identification or Simulation steps. Therefore, the total mental preparation sessions are relatively fewer.

5. The intervention programs are flexible and the athlete's progress is documented using objective measurements such as time, physiological measures (e.g., GSR, EMG), direction of change, and norms.
6. The process of acquiring psychological techniques/strategies is developed through three stages: learning, modified, and applied.
7. The intervention programs allows for input and the cooperation with the coach.

In the following chapters our intervention programs will be described in detail, while they are applied in a variety of case studies of athletes from different sport disciplines and of skill levels.

REFERENCES

Balague, G.(2000). Periodization of psychological skills training. *Journal of Science and Medicine in Sport*, 3, 230-237.

Bar-Eli, M., Lurie,Y., and Breivik ,G. (1999). Rationality in sport: A psychophilosophical approach. In R.Lidor and M.Bar-Eli (Eds.), *Sport psychology: Linking theory and practice* (pp.35-58). Morgantown, WV: Fitness Information Technology.

Blumenstein, B. (2001). Sport psychology practice in two cultures: Similarities and differences. In G. Tenenbaum (Ed.), The practice of sport psychology (pp. 231-240). Morgantown, WV: Fitness Information Technology.

Blumenstein, B., and Bar-Eli, M. (2005). Biofeedback applications in sport. In D. Hackfort, J. Duda, and R. Lidor (Eds.). *Handbook of research in applied sport and exercise psychology: International perspectives* (pp. 185-198). Morgantown, WV. Fitness Information Technology.

Blumenstein, B., Bar-Eli, M., and Collins, D. (2002). Biofeedback training in sport. In B. Blumenstein, M. Bar-Eli, and G. Tenenbaum (Eds.), *Brain and body in sport and exercise: Biofeedback applications in performance enhancement* (pp. 55-76). Chichester, UK: Wiley.

Blumenstein, B., Bar-Eli, M., and Tenenbaum, G. (1997). A five step approach to mental training incorporating biofeedback. *The Sport Psychologist, 11*, 440-453.

Blumenstein, B., and Lidor, R. (2004). Psychological preparation in elite canoeing and kayaking sport programs: Periodization and planning. *Applied Research in Coaching and Athletics Annual, 19*, 24-34.

Blumenstein, B., and Lidor, R. (2007). The road to the Olympic Games: Four-years psychological preparation program. *Athletic Insight: The Online Journal of Sport Psychology, 9(4)*.

Blumenstein, B., and Lidor, R. (2008). Psychological preparation it the Olympic village: Four-phase approach. *International Journal of Sport and Exercise Psychology, 6,* 287-300.

Blumenstein, B., Lidor, R., and Tenenbaum, G. (2005). Periodization and planning of psychological preparation in elite combat sport programs: The case of Judo. *International Journal of Sport and Exercise Psychology, 3,* 7-25.

Blumenstein, B., and Orbach, I. (2011, in press). The road to Olympic medal. In A. Edmonds and G. Tenenbaum (Eds.), Case studies in applied psychophysiology: Neurofeedback and biofeedback treatments for advanced in human performance. Chichester:West Sussex, Wiley-Blackwell.

Blumenstein, B., Tenenbaum, G., Bar-Eli, M., and Pie, J. (1995). Mental preparation techniques with elite athletes using computerized biofeedback and VCR. *Applied Research in Coaching and Athletics Annual*, 1,1-16.

Blumenstein, B. and Weinstein, Y. (2010). *Psychological skills training: Application to elite sport performance.* Grand Rapids, MI: Ultimate Athlete Concepts.

Bompa, T. (1999). *Periodization: Theory and methodology of training* (4th ed.). Champaign, IL: Human Kinetics.

Carrera, M., and Bompa, T. (2007). Theory and methodology of training: General perspectives. In B. Blumenstein, R. Lidor, and G. Tenenbaum (Eds.). *Psychology of sport training* (pp. 19-39). Oxford, UK: Meyer and Meyer Sport.

Frey, M., Laguna, P. L., and Ravizza, K. (2003). Collegiate athletes' mental skill use and perceptions of success: An exploration of the practice and competition settings. *Journal of Applied Sport Psychology*, *15,* 115-128.

Gould, D. (2001). Goal setting for peak performance. In J. Williams (Ed.), *Applied sport psychology: Personal growth to peak performance* (4th ed., pp. 190-205). Mountain View, CA: Mayfield Publishing Company.

Gould, D. (2002). The psychology of Olympic excellence and its development. *Psychology, 9*, 531-546.

Henschen, K. (2005). Mental practice-skill oriented. In D. Hackfort, J. Duda, and R. Lidor (Eds.), *Handbook of research in applied sport and exercise psychology: International perspective*s (pp. 19-36). Morgantown, WV: Fitness Information Technology.

Holliday, B., Burton, D., Sun, G., Hammermeister, J., Naylor, S., and Friegang, D. (2008). Building the better mental training mousetrap: Is periodization a more systematic approach to promoting performance excellence? *Journal of Applied Sport Psychology, 20(2)*, 199-219.

Hung, T. M., Lidor, R., and Hackfort, D. (Eds.). (2009). *Psychology of sport excellence*. Morgantown, WV: Fitness Information Technology.

Issurin, V. B. (2007). A modern approach to high-performance training: The block composition concept. In B. Blumenstein, R. Lidor, and G. Tenenbaum (Eds.). *Psychology of sport training* (pp. 216-234). Oxford, UK: Meyer and Meyer Sport.

Kondo, C. V., Canter, J. A., and Bean, J. H. (1977). Intersession interval and reductions in frontalis EMG during biofeedback training. *Psychophysiology, 1,* 15-17.

Landers, D. M., Petruzzello, S. J., Salazar, W., Crews, D. L., Kubitz, K. A., Gannon, T. L., and Han, M. (1991). The influence of electrocortical biofeedback on performance in pre-elite archers. *Medicine and Science in Sport and Exercise, 23*, 123-129.

Lidor, R. (2010). Pre-performance routines. In S. Hanrahan and M. Andersen (Eds.), *Routledge handbook of applied sport psychology: A comprehensive guide for students and practitioners* (pp. 537-546). London and New York: Routledge Taylor and Francis Group.

Lidor, R., and Bar-Eli, M. (1998). Physical education in Israel: An overview. *Chronicle of Physical Education in Higher Education, 9*, 7, 14-15.

Lidor, R., and Blumenstein, B. (2009). Working with elite athletes in Israel. In R. Schinke S. Hanrahan (Eds.). *Cultural sport psychology* (pp. 141-152). Champaign, IL: Human Kinetics.

Lidor, R., Blumenstein, B., and Tenenbaum, G. (2007). Psychological aspects of training programs in European basketball: Conceptualization, periodization and planning. *The Sport Psychologist, 21*, 353-367.

Lidor, R., Blumenstein, B., and Tenenbaum, G. (2009). Periodization and planning of psychological preparation in individual and team sports. In B. Blumenstein, R. Lidor, and G. Tenenbaum (Eds.). *Psychology of sport training* (pp. 137-161). Oxford, UK: Meyer and Meyer Sport.

Lidor, R., and Singer, R. (2005). Learning strategies in motor skill acquisition: From laboratory to the gym. In D. Hackfort, J. Duda, and R. Lidor (Eds.). *Handbook of research in applied sport and exercise psychology: International perspectives* (pp. 109-126). Morgantown, WV: Fitness Information Technology.

Moran, A. (2010). Concentrations/attention. In S. Hanrahan and M. Andersen (Eds.), *Routledge handbook of applied sport psychology: A comprehensive guide for students and practitioners* (pp. 500-509). London and New York: Routledge Taylor and Francis Group.

Moran, A. (2005). Training attention and concentration skills in athletes. In D. Hackfort, J. Duda, and R. Lidor (Eds.). *Handbook of research in applied sport and exercise psychology: International perspectives* (pp. 61-74). Morgantown, WV: Fitness Information Technology.

Morris, T. (2010). Imagery. In S. Hanrahan and M. Andersen (Eds.), *Routledge handbook of applied sport psychology: A comprehensive guide for students and practitioners* (pp. 481-489). London and New York: Routledge Taylor and Francis Group.

Pedro, J., and Durbin, W. (2001) *Judo: Techniques and tactics*. Champaign, IL: Human Kinetics.

Schultz, J. H., (1932). *Das autogene training* (Autogenic Training). Stuttgart, Germany: Thieme.

Tenenbaum, G., and Bar-Eli, M. (1993). Decision making in sport: A cognitive perspective. In R. Singer, M. Murphey, and K. Tennant (Eds.). *Handbook on research in sport psychology* (pp. 171-192). New York: McMillan.

Smith, D. (2003).A framework for understanding the training process leading to elite performance. *Sports Medicine, 33*(5), 1103-1126.

Vealey, R. (2007). Mental skills training in sport. In G. Tenenbaum and R. Eklund (Eds.). *Handbook of sport psychology* (3rd ed.; pp. 287-309). New York: Wiley.

Weinberg, R. (2010). Activation/arousal control. In S. Hanrahan and M. Andersen (Eds.), *Routledge handbook of applied sport psychology: A comprehensive guide for students and practitioners* (pp. 471-480). London and New York: Routledge Taylor and Francis Group.

Weinberg, R., and Butt, J. (2005). Goal setting in sport and exercise domains: The theory and practice of effective goal setting. In D. Hackfort, J. Duda, and R. Lidor (Eds.), *Handbook of research in applied sport and exercise psychology: International perspectives* (pp. 129-146). Morgantown, WV: Fitness Information Technology.

Weinberg, R. S., and Comar, W. (1994). The effectiveness of psychological interventions in competitive sport. *Sports Medicine Journal, 18*, 406-418.

Williams, J. and Krane, V. (2001). Psychological characteristics of peak performance. In J. Williams (Ed.), *Applied sport psychology: Personal growth to peak performance* (4th ed., pp. 162-178). Mountain View, CA: Mayfield Publishing Company.

Zatsiorsky, V. M. (1995). *Science and practice of strength training.* Champaign, IL: Human Kinetics.

Chapter 2

PSYCHOLOGICAL SKILLS TRAINING IN COMBAT SPORTS

ABSTRACT

This chapter describes psychological aspects of peak performance in combat sport and focuses on psychological skills training (PST) with elite combat athletes from judo, taekwondo, and fencing. PST is an important component of the combat athletes' preparation, but it is only a part of their overall training. The PST program used in each of the four case studies described in this chapter is based on the periodization principle. In addition, a similar intervention program was used with those athletes before international competitions. The differing variables between the case studies are the time frame of cooperation with the sport psychology consultant, the continuity of the PST, the specific sport, and the gender of the athlete.

INTRODUCTION

Psychological skills training (PST) has been found to be a significant factor in the athlete's success, together with physical, tactical, and technical factors (Bompa, 1999; Carrera and Bompa, 2007; Weinberg and Williams, 2006). The success of the mental preparation practiced in PST is usually evaluated based on the athlete's achievements in competition. The first author (BB) relates an anecdotal story from 1992, while he was a sport psychologist of the National Judo Team, taking his first steps working with Israeli athletes following his extensive experience working with former Soviet Union elite athletes (Blumenstein, 2001). At one of the European competitions, one of the athletes won his first match. He celebrated his victory with jumping and singing together with the rest of the Israeli delegation, as if he had won an Olympic gold medal. BB was amazed by this reaction, since it was just the beginning of the competition, and he asked the athlete to give the reason for his happiness and to explain why he was not getting prepared for the next match. The athlete's response was: "I won the match. My trip here was not wasted – I did what I had to do." This reaction characterizes the athlete's low expectations for himself. Today, as a result of expanded scientific knowledge, improved medical services, and extensive training, our athletes' standards and motivation are different. Therefore our goal and vision for success is determined by medals and finals in the European and World levels, and not merely by participation. Throughout the years our athletes were happy just to participation, and maybe to win one match. This is an indication of the improvement in the different fields of the training process, encompassing the areas of scientific and medical services.

Psychological Characteristics of Combat Sport: Competition in elite combat sports requires quick responses as well as high levels of attention, self-control, consistency, and will power (Blumenstein, Lidor, and Tenenbaum, 2005; Pedro and Durbin, 2001). Combat situations may often change within extremely short periods of time (e.g., 100 to 200 msec); accordingly, emotional and mental states are subject to extreme fluctuation during combat matches. It is difficult for the competing athlete to simultaneously attack and defend while concealing his/her intentions from the opponent, and while in an extreme state of tension; it is not easy to make decisions under time pressure while facing aggressive opponents, and to decide on alternative tactical movements (i.e., attention flexibility) – all while striving to achieve the designated goals (Blumenstein, Bar-Eli, and Collins, 2002; Blumenstein et al., 2005; Pedro and Durbin, 2001).

In order for psychological preparation for combat sports to be effective, it must target specific physical, technical, and tactical preparations. In addition, the duration of the competition plays a critical role in the psychological preparation. For example, a judo match lasts 5 min (for both men and women); a taekwondo match lasts three rounds, and each round lasts for 2 minutes with a 1-min pause in between. In our psychological training programs for elite athletes in combat sports, the duration of the training exercises is identical to the length of the competition, so that laboratory/field discrepancies are minimal. Our PST program is based on the periodization principle – a conceptual framework for improving athlete's performance (Blumenstein and

Lidor, 2008; Blumenstein et al., 2005; Blumenstein and Orbach, 2011, in press; Holliday et al., 2008). The PST contents and the direction of each mental session are integrated with physical training. We developed norms and demands for the athletes' mental performance in each preparation phase, which were used by the coach and the athlete as a reference point to evaluate mental improvement. Moreover, these tools improved coach-athlete-sport psychology consultant relationships and the integration of mental practice as a significant component of the overall training process.

In judo, among the psychological skills that are important are confidence, anticipation, concentration, self-talking, and self-control (Anshel and Payne, 2006; Blumenstein et al., 2005). Similarly, the psychological skills for taekwondo are self-control, concentration, self-confidence, anticipation, and competitiveness (Anshel and Payne, 2006; Blumenstein et al., 2005).

Lastly, the mental preparation of fencers includes the developing of reasoning (interpretation) skills, such as concentration, self-control, relaxation, and self-talking (Blumenstein, and Weinstein, 2010). To summarize, combat athletes usually function under dynamic situations which demand various uses of cognitive processes, such as anticipating movements made by the opponent, making decisions, and executing the planned act. The combat athlete is expected to be able to respond swiftly with high levels of attention, consistency, and stability. Several cases of combat athletes will be discussed below.

CASE 1: JUDO – TEN YEARS OF COOPERATION BETWEEN AN ATHLETE AND SPORT PSYCHOLOGY CONSULTANT

Judoka A. became well-known from a very young age. His first international medal was achieved when he was only 15 years old – a gold medal in the World Junior Championship (1992). Up to the senior level, the judoka achieved all of his medals from youth European and World Championships. In 1997, at a senior judo World Championship, the athlete achieved only seventh place. During 1998 Judoka A. had no significant competition achievements. The athlete was not stable, with low sport motivation, low self-confidence, and bad moods and he did not have any clear vision about his sport future. However, he heard about a sport psychology consultant that worked intensively with one of the combat athletes (wrestling) at the Wingate Institute. As a result, the athlete approached the sport

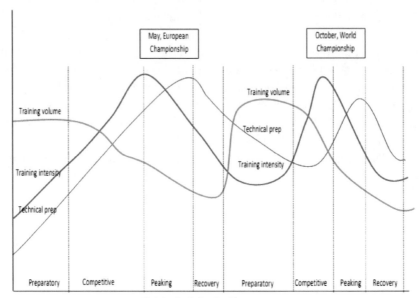

Figure 2.1. Double Peaking (Bi-cycle) of the Annual Training Plan in Judo.

psychology consultant (the first author; BB) and asked for his help. He and BB
started their joint work in September 1998. BB called several general meetings
with the athlete and the coach, visited the athlete's training sessions in order to
understand the atmosphere and the coach-athlete relationship, and based on
that developed together with the coach tentative short and long term goals. It
was obvious that the athlete had to achieve significant results in the next year
in the senior group at the European championship (May, 1999) and World
Championship (October, 1999). Therefore, our mental work was developed
around these two peaking events.

Preparation Phase (PP)

In the PP the meetings took place starting with one per week, which lasted
50-60 minutes. In the first two meetings BB took time to improve the athlete's
mood, motivation, and self-confidence by using simple concentration exercises
and BFB games, with which he was able to achieve success. During future
sessions, muscle relaxation, imagery, and concentration exercises were
accompanied by Electromyography/Galvanic Skin Response Biofeedback
(EMG/GSR BFB) devices. In the general preparation of the PP, the athlete

mastered the first two steps of the Wingate 5-Step Approach (W5SA) in a relatively short period of time: The first step lasted for 6 meetings (September-October), and the second step lasted for seven meetings (November-December). His first Self-Regulation Test (SRT) result was 5-6+. In the next two months (special preparation) the meetings were used to improve self-talk, concentration with GSR control, motivation, and self-confidence. At the end of December BB and the athlete started to work with the Reaction Training Program (RTP) (see Chapter 1). In the first two sessions the athlete practiced a Reaction Training (RT) task (15 simple - 30 choice – 30 discrimination) and achieved the following results: 202 msc – 221 msc – 214 msc, respectively. His behavioral style during the RTP was not effective: High muscle tension during and between the reactions, rigid in his body reactions, concentration not optimal for the specific exercise, and wrong decision making, and therefore he was exhausted at the end of the sessions (Blumenstein and Weinstein, 2010). Based on that BB realized that much work needed to be done in order to bring about significant progress. Therefore BB, together with the athlete and the coach, decided to extend the mental training to twice a week: One meeting (Monday) for RTP and concentration, and the second meeting (Thursday) for BFB training (W5SA) and imagery. After returning from a two-week training camp in Japan at the beginning of January, we continued our mutual work using the twice-a-week model.

In February the results of the RT task were 175msc – 185msc – 190msc, and SRT results 8-9+, and his relaxation ability improved significantly (short relaxation 1-3 minutes). A concentration exercise with GSR BFB was Δ50-100kΩ during a 20-sec interval. The athlete successfully applied his "lab" skills during training: fast ability to concentrate, relaxation-excitation waves, and self-talk. During our meetings the athlete said "You know, it is working. I began to be relaxed in the match, I am fast." The athlete's mood and sport motivation significantly improved, together with his self-confidence.

Competition Phase (CP)

This phase took place during the months February-May, 1999, with the main objective being success in the European championship in May 1999. During this period our main goals were to strengthen the athlete's mental skills, which were developed by the W5SA, the RTP, and the Specific Psychological Training Program (SPTP) while being exposed to different levels of stressful factors (see Chapter 1).In April the athlete achieved 155msc

– 175msc – 170msc (with competition noises) in RTP; his ability to concentrate was fast, and his relaxation-excitation control was accurate and fast. BB developed his pre-competition routine, and practiced its impact and effectiveness in several competitions. From April to mid-May, about 20 imagery "matches" with potential European opponents were provided. Each match was practiced with competition noises and competitive films of the athlete and his opponents. In the end, the athlete had a concrete mental plan per each opponent. In May 1999, during the European championship, the athlete achieved his first senior bronze medal.

Transition Phase (TP)

During this short phase the athlete recovered for 10 days at a spa in Eilat, and had two weeks of low volume and intensive training. Two relaxation sessions with BFB games and music were provided in this phase.

Approximately the same preparation model was used in the second mesocycle, with minor corrections such as a shorter time for training in the W5SA, RTP and SPTP. The athlete achieved fifth place in the World Senior Judo Championship (1999). During the year 1999 we acquired good experience in mental preparation for combat sport. The athlete's motivation and self-confidence were high. We started the year of 2000, the Olympic Year, with great optimism and hope. During that season we used the same PST program with the W5SA, RTP, and the SPTP, with relevant norm correction: For example, W5SA: Shorter training on steps 2, 3, and 4; RTP: Higher norms for RT tasks and balance between fast and slow reaction. In the athlete's first Olympic Games (Sydney, 2000), he achieved respectable fifth place.

The next eight-year period (two Olympic cycles) was well-defined and planned, with more specific mental interventions and higher norms for combat sports (Blumenstein and Lidor, 2008; Blumenstein et al., 2005).

BB and judoka A. finished their joint work before the 2008 Beijing Olympic Games (May, 2008) according to the coach's decision (see Table 2.1).

This case illustrates a successful 10-year period of cooperation with a combat athlete, integrating PST in the training process and developing a PST model for combat sport, in which psychological interventions were modified according to the sport's demands. PST was provided in a systematic, stable manner and was a real part of athlete's general preparation.

Table 2.1. Athletes Achievements throughout 2001-2011

	2001	2002	2003	2004	2005	2006	2007	2008[*]	2009[*]	2010[*]	2011[*]
European Champ.	1st	5th	1st	1st	2nd		3rd	3rd	5th	3rd	7th
World Champ.	2nd (open w.)	5th	–	1st (Olympic qualified champ.)	3rd (World Cup)		–	1st in World Cup		won one match	won one match
Olympic Games	–	–	–	3rd	–		–	won one match			

[*] During this year the athlete did not work with BB.

CASE 2: JUDO – NON-SYSTEMATIC START FOLLOWED BY TWO YEARS OF WORK

The judoka R., one of Israel's best combat athletes, immigrated to Israel at the age of 11 in 1991. He learned and trained in the Youth Sport Academy at the Wingate Institute, and took part in different national and international junior levels, and from 2000 in senior competitions. In addition to this athlete, most of the National judo team worked with BB. At first judoka R. said, "I don't need help. I am strong with good will and high motivation". However, BB believed the athlete would benefit from mental training intervention, but the athlete did not believe he needed any psychological assistance. As a matter of fact, this athlete had a strong character, had faced many injuries and comebacks to training, and experienced problems finding a suitable coach. Until 2004 the athlete did not achieve significant results in international competitions.

In February 2002 the athlete approached BB and asked for his help to get ready for the European Championship in May 2002. BB replied that he usually recommended on a stable work person lasting that last for at least a year. However, BB agreed to accept the athlete, with the demand that for the rest of the three months the athlete must come for mental training twice a week. The meetings were based on two models. The first model included RTP and concentration exercises. An example for one meeting, which was provided as part of the first model, is as follows:

Monday, 13:00-14:00, Laboratory:

1. Concentration exercise with GSR BFB 10 x 20 sec, 10 x 10 sec.
2. RTP: (Simple-10; Choice-20: Discrimination-20) x 2 times
     (Simple-15; Choice-30: Discrimination-30) x 3 times
3. Relaxation with EMG/GSR BFB for 5 min.

Starting in April, the above exercises were practiced while being exposed to various levels of stress factors (see Chapter 1).

The second model included the W5SA (short versions of the first, second, and third steps) and imagery competition matches with different levels of stressful factors. An example for one meeting, which was provided as part of the second model, is as follows:

Thursday, 13:00-14:00, Laboratory:

1. The first step of W5SA (short version).
2. Imagery of matches with possible European opponents: 3-4 times x 5 min. During the imagery the athlete signals with his fingers attack movements.
3. Concentration exercises 10-15 times x 10, 20 sec.
4. Relaxation with BFB games.

In April, about six weeks before the competitive event, all the above exercises were practiced while the athlete was being exposed to different levels of stressful factors.

In April, approximately one week before the competition, the athlete achieved the following results (see Table 2.2). For comparison purposes, the athlete's results from the beginning of the intervention in February are presented as well.

The athlete improved his self-regulation, concentration, and reaction-time skills from February to April, as can be seen in the SRT and RTP results, although in April the results were taken while the athlete was being exposed to different levels of stressful factors. Moreover, movement quality improved, as can be seen in the ratio between fast and slow reaction time. In May, the athlete for the first time achieved a respectful fifth place in the European Championship, in Germany.

At the end of July 2003, two months before the World Championship, the judoka came to BB's laboratory and asked to continue the mental support. To BB's question of why the athlete did not work systematically on his mental skills, the athlete replied: "I already know the skills. I just need to refresh my

Table 2.2. The athlete's results in SRT and RTP in the Beginning of the Intervention vs. before Competition

February	April
SRT results: 6+	SRT results: 9+
RTP (15-30-30):	RTP (15-30-30):
• simple 195 (with ratio of 7 fast and 8 slow)	• simple 175 (with ratio of 9 fast and 6 slow)
• choice 215 (with ratio of 5 fast and 10 slow)	• choice 180 (with ratio of 8 fast and 7 slow)
• discrimination 190 (with ratio of 6 fast and 9 slow)	• discrimination 165 (with ratio of 9 fast and 6 slow)

memory before the World Championship". Although BB was not "happy" with this response, he worked together with the athlete on the same model as previously. The athlete and BB agreed that after the World Championship they would seriously start their joint work.

The athlete achieved a respectful seventh place in the World Championship, September 2003, Japan.

From October 2003, the athlete and BB started joint systematical work, which was based on the periodization principle (see Case 1 and Table 2.3). The three basic sub-programs which on we focused during the psychological training were W5SA, RTP, and SPTP (see Chapter 1). During the *Preparatory Phase* (October-December, 2003), the first two steps of the W5SA were applied. In addition, as part of the RTP, the typical workload was 15-30-30 with no stress factor. SPTP strategies such as concentration exercise and imagery were modified based on the sport's demands (imagery time changed from 3 to 5 min to reflect a real-life match). In addition, the goals were modified from long-term training goals to short-term performance goals. In the *Competitive Phase* (February-May, 2004), they worked on steps 3, 4, and 5, which were related to dealing with competitive and training stressors. In RTP the workload was shorter (10-20-20) and included stress factors. SPTP strategies were modified to reflect more specifically competitive factors. For example, imagery and concentration exercise included stress factors, goal settings focused on technical and tactical goals, and precompetitive routine included strategies, game plans, and key words. In the *Transition Phase* two relaxation sessions with music were provided.

Judoka R. and BB worked together for two years (2004-2005). During this time the athlete achieved second place in the European Championship, Romania 2004, met the Olympic criterion, and had honorable results (two victories) in Olympic events. BB remembers that one day before the European Championship the athlete came to BB's hotel room and asked him to check his RTP abilities. BB hesitated but decided to take the risk. The results of the RTP (10-20-20) were: 143 (9/1), 168 (8/2), and 135 (10/0). The judoka had achieved his best results, but he was suspicious about the reliability of the equipment (computer). After taking a walk, the athlete went to sleep, and the next day during his match he was very focused, aggressive, and confident. Eventually, the athlete achieved his first silver medal. In 2005 the athlete achieved second place in the European championship, Holland, and numerous medals in tournaments "A". In 2006 the athlete decided to train on his own. In the subsequent years the athlete did not have any significant achievements.

Table 2.3. Example of Psychological Skill Training Schedule with Judoka R. (First Mesocycle)

	W5SA	RTP	Psychological Techniques/Strategies SPTP				
			Concentration Exercise	Imagery	Relaxation	Goal Setting	Precompetitive Routine
Preparatory Phase: October, 2003	1st step	(15-30-30)x3 times	10x 20-30sec	3x3min	10-15min	Long and short term goals	Develop self-talk
November, 2003	1st–2nd steps	(15-30-30)x3 times	10x 20-30sec with GSR BFB	3x4min	10-15min	Short term goals; daily practice goals	Self talk before and during practice
SP December, 2003	2nd step	(15-30-30)x3 times	10x 20-30sec with GSR BFB	3x5min	10-15min	Goals for positive thinking	Stop negative thoughts
January, 2004	Training Camp in Japan						
Competitive Phase: February, 2004	3rd step	(15-30-30)x3 times+ stress distraction (b, c)	10x 10sec with GSR BFB+ stress distraction (a, b, c)	IM+VCR 3x5min	5-10min	Performance goals; positive thinking	Stop negative thoughts; self-talk during practice

Table 2.3. (Continued)

	W5SA	RTP	Psychological Techniques/Strategies SPTP				
			Concentration Exercise	Imagery	Relaxation	Goal Setting	Precompetitive Routine
March, 2004	3rd-4th steps	(10-20-20)x3 times+ stress distraction (d, f)	10x 10sec with GSR BFB+ stress distraction (d, e, f)	IM+VCR 3x5min	5-10 min	Technical and tactical goals	Preperformance routine
April, 2004	4th-5th steps	(10-20-20)x3 times+ stress distraction (e, f)	10x 10sec with GSR BFB+ stress distraction (e, f)	IM+VCR 3x5min	5-10 min	Performance, technical, tactical goals	Precompetitive routine (strategies, game plan, concentration, key words)
May, 2004		(10-20-20)x3 times+ stress distraction (e, f)	10x 10sec with GSR BFB+ stress distraction (e, f)	IM+VCR 3x5min	5-10 min	Major events strategy goals	Precompetitive routine (strategies, game plan, concentration, key words)
Transition Phase: June, 2004					5-10 min		

In this case we used the same PST model, which helped the judoka to achieve significant sport results in his weight category. The athlete was very optimistic and motivated during this training period. Unfortunately, due to personal reasons, the athlete could not continue this successful support. The future performances of this athlete indicated that in this case PST had been a significant factor in his personal development.

CASE 3: TAEKWONDO – ONE-YEAR COOPERATION BEFORE EUROPEAN CHAMPIONSHIP

Athlete T. was well-known in the country during his participation at the youth level (1999: third place in the European championship; 2000: third place in the World Championship). When the athlete started to compete at the senior level, he was placed number 2-3 on the national team, but did not achieve any significant results during the next four years. In 2004, the athlete's major opponent from the national team left the country to study abroad. As a consequence, T. found himself as the main athlete in his weight category. Together with the coach, the athlete came to BB's laboratory and asked to work with him on a systematic basis to get prepared for the next European Championship in Germany (2006). After observations and evaluations, BB recommended the following model: Meetings with the consultant in the laboratory twice a week, consultant visit practice 1-2 times per week, and taking a part in 2-3 competitions (one local and one abroad). The PST was based on the periodization principle and included the short version of the W5SA, RTP, and SPTP. According to the sport's demands (match lasting 3 rounds x 2 min, with a 1-min pause), BB modified the sub-programs. For example, training of the steps of the W5SA was shorter; relaxation exercises lasted for only 30sec-1min to be used during the 1-min pause in the match, etc. Imagery was provided during the second meeting of each week, and lasted 3 rounds x 2 min. During the competitive phase we exposed the athlete to different stress factors (see Figure 2.2). The levels of difficulty started from the easiest level which is the "ordinary laboratory setting", and ended up with the level of "various combinations". For more details regarding the stress factor scale, see Chapter 1. The following book is also recommended: "Psychological skills training: Application to elite sport performance", by Blumenstein and Weinstein (2010).

7. Various combinations of levels 1-6

6. Performance under "true" competition noise

5. Performance under "true" competition sights

4. Reward/punishment for performance

3. Performance under precise demands

2. Verbal motivation: Positive/negative

1. Ordinary laboratory settings

Figure 2.2. Scale of stress factors applied in PST with athletes.

According to BB's request, the athlete brought his coach to the consultant meetings, and during the competitive phase BB asked the coach to make comments to the athlete during imagery to imitate a real-life match. The cooperation with the coach during the consultant sessions was the uniqueness of this case. In this method, the athlete is exposed to specific professional comments against concrete opponents. The athlete was able to deal with critical situations as they are in the real world, and as consequences he felt more confident and ready. The athlete, by using imagery strategies, planned and readied himself for his main European opponents.

His main achievement during this period was a silver medal in the European Senior Taekwondo Championship, 2006 (see Table 2.4). From 2007 the athlete continued to train with his coach without any psychological support. The main reason for discontinuing the consultation was the difficulty of arriving at the Wingate Institute; the athlete had to take two buses in order to get to BB's office. The athlete did not achieve significant results after he finished the consultation meetings with BB.

The data illustrate the importance of the psychological support on an athlete's achievements, and it can serve as a professional promotion for psychological preparation in the training process. At present, the athlete

Table 2.4. The Athlete's Achievement Throughout 1999-2009

Year	Category	Tournament	Achievement
1999	Under 55kg Youth male	European Championship	3
2000	Under 59kg Youth male	World Championship	3
2001	Under 62kg Male	World Championship	16
2004	Under 67kg Male	European Championship	8
2005	Under 67kg Male	World Championship	16
2005	Under 67kg Male	European Championship	8
2006[*]	Under 67kg Male	European Championship	2
2007	Under 67kg Male	World Championship	32
2007	Under 67kg Male	Universiade	16
2008	Under 67kg Male	European Championship	8
2009	Under 68kg Male	World Championship	32

[*] 2006 was the only year the athlete worked with BB.

acknowledged the significant effect of the mental factor on his results. However, especially in sport, there is a narrow window of opportunity for best performance, which in this case was not fulfilled.

CASE 4: FENCING – FROM SYSTEMATIC COOPERATION TO PERIODIC MEETINGS WITH A FEMALE ATHLETE

In 2004, the fencer M. came to BB's office together with her coach. During that time the athlete was not part of the national team and was ranked in fourth-fifth place in the country. The coach asked BB to start working with the athlete and to assist her to achieve better results. After the Athens Olympic

Games we initiated the consultation sessions. The same techniques, strategies, and principles were used during our two-year systematic work and later at periodic meetings. During the systematic work BB adjusted the requirements based on the demands of her sport (fencing). For example, a shorter version of the W5SA, RTP (10-20-20 and 5-10-10), and SPTP were modified based on fencing's demands: Concentration exercises were shorter (5, 10 sec); relaxation-excitation waves between matches; imagery was based on competition scenes in the pool (group-matches 5-points) and direct elimination (knockout, 15-points match); long relaxation between matches; and self-talk with tactical orientation during match. Some of the imagery was provided with the coach's participation, including his comments during the imagery, especially with tactical recommendations in a match against a concrete opponent. All work was based on the periodization principle. The athlete progressed up to the point that her results in the RTP were the best achieved by a professional female athlete who worked with BB. More specifically, in the Simple RT the athlete's result was less than 102 ms with ratio of 8/2; in the Choice RT she achieved 107 ms with a ratio of 9/1, and in the Discrimination 102 ms with ratio of 9/1. The fencer coped with different stress factors and performed RTP under positive/negative motivation: simple RT 130/101, choice RT 129/118 and discrimination RT 106/109.

Our periodic consultations were provided according to the coach and/or the fencer's request. Usually, the fencer met with BB 6-8 times during one-two month period before a major competition. The main objectives of the sessions were to:

1. Refine the link between concentration and muscle relaxation skills under stress by using RTP with different stress factors.
2. Develop and improve a tactical plan against concrete opponents by using imagery, self-talk, and performance goals.
3. Improve concentration skills before fights and relaxation skills between fights.
4. Develop self-confidence before significant competitions by using SRT, RTP, and self-talking.

In 2007, the athlete was accepted to Harvard University for academic studies. However, she deferred her admittance in order to train for the 2008 Beijing Olympics Games. To conclude this case, we need to mark the positive and important role her coach performed throughout all the periods of our cooperation.

**Table 2.5. Athlete's Achievements during Psychological
Consultation Support**

Year	Achievement	Competition
2005	10	Junior World Championship, Austria
2006	11	European Championship, Turkey
2007	2	World University Games, Thailand
2008	7	European Championship, Ukraine
	22	Olympic Games, China
2009	7	European Championship, Bulgaria
2010	3	European Championship, Germany

CONCLUSION

To summarize this chapter, there are several conclusions that can be presented.

In the four cases discussed, PST was based on the periodization principle and was linked with the training process. Three sub-programs were used: the W5SA, RTP, and SPTP.

There was positive cooperation with the coach, which was a significant factor for the continuation of the psychological support. Once the coach was not obligated to this support due to various reasons, the cooperation between the athlete and the consultant was usually terminated. This led to a negative effect on the athlete's achievements. On the other hand, with the coach's cooperation, long-term, systematic psychological support led to positive results.

REFERENCES

Anshel, M., and Payne, J. M. (2006). Application of sport psychology for optimal performance in martial arts. In J. Dosil (Ed.),*The sport psychologist's handbook: A guide for sport-specific performance enhancement* (pp. 353-374). Chichester, UK: Wiley.

Blumenstein, B. (2001). Sport psychology practice in two cultures: Similarities and differences. In G. Tenenbaum (Ed.), The practice of sport psychology (pp. 231-240). Morgantown, WV: Fitness Information Technology.

Blumenstein, B., Bar-Eli, M., and Collins, D. (2002). Biofeedback training in sport. In B. Blumenstein, M. Bar-Eli, and G. Tenenbaum (Eds.). *Brain and body in sport and exercise: Biofeedback applications in performance enhancement* (pp. 55-76). Chichester, UK: Wiley.

Blumenstein, B., and Lidor, R. (2008). Psychological preparation in the Olympic village: Four-phase approach. *International Journal of Sport and Exercise Psychology, 6*, 287-300.

Blumenstein, B., Lidor, R., and Tenenbaum, G. (2005). Periodization and planning of psychological preparation in elite combat sport programs: The case of judo. *International Journal of Sport and Exercise Psychology, 3*, 7-25.

Blumenstein, B., and Orbach, I. (2011, in press). The road to Olympic medal. In A. Edmonds and G. Tenenbaum (Eds.), Case studies in applied psychophysiology: Neurofeedback and biofeedback treatments for advances in human performance. Chichester,West Sussex: Wiley-Blackwell.

Blumenstein, B., and Weinstein, Y. (2010). *Psychological skills training: Application to elite sport performance.* Grand Rapids, MI: Ultimate Athlete Concepts.

Bompa, T. (1999). *Periodization: Theory and methodology of training* (4th ed.). Champaign, IL: Human Kinetics.

Carrera, M., and Bompa, T. (2007). Theory and methodology of training: General perspectives. In B. Blumenstein, R. Lidor, and G. Tenenbaum (Eds.), *Psychology of sport training* (pp. 19-39). Oxford, UK: Meyer and Meyer Sport.

Holliday, B., Burton, D., Sun, G., Hammermeister, J., Naylor, S., and Friegang, D. (2008). Building the better mental training mousetrap: Is periodization a more systematic approach to promoting performance excellence? *Journal of Applied Sport Psychology, 20*(2), 199-219.

Pedro, J. and Durbin, W. (2001). *Judo: Techniques and tactics.* Champaign, IL: Human Kinetics.

Weinberg, R., and Williams, J. (2006). Integrating and implementing a psychological skills training program. In J. Williams (Ed.), *Applied sport psychology: Personal growth to peak performance* (5th ed., pp. 425-457). Mountain View, CA: Mayfield.

Chapter 3

PSYCHOLOGICAL SKILLS TRAINING IN INDIVIDUAL SPORTS

ABSTRACT

In the third chapter the authors focus on five cases from individual sports: rhythmic gymnastics, pole vault, kayaking, windsurfing and swimming. In the first four cases the authors used similar Psychological Skills Training (PST) periodization, which included intensive and systematic work in the preparation phase (1-2 times per week in the lab and 1-2 times per week in training), and periodic intensive work in the competitive phase before a significant competition (usually during a one-month training camp at the Wingate Institute; twice per week in the lab and every day in training). This type of work schedule was used due to the fact that most of the athletes' training and competitions during the year took place abroad. In addition, the chapter includes an explanation on how the authors plan an annual and a weekly PST program, both in the lab and in the field.

INTRODUCTION

In individual sports the athletes attempt to achieve excellence by hard and solitary training. The athletes rely only on their own physical and psychological abilities while competing against an opponent. In this chapter we present a specific model for the design and implementation of an educational psychological skills program for individual sport. This program includes laboratory and field mental training sessions which prepare the athlete for significant competition, such as the European Championship and Olympic Games. Moreover, as part of our PST program we planned collaboration between athletes from various individual sport disciplines and along different training periods. For example, in the preparation phase the athletes from gymnastics and pole vault sometimes warmed up together, especially for stretching exercises and acrobatic preparation. This led to positive energy in the gymnasts and athletes, raised motivation and let to a better mood during the routine exercises, which included many repetitions and monotonous work. In addition, the kayaker and the pole vaulter worked out together during strength exercises. The windsurfing case is unique, due to the setting where most of the psychological work took place: from laboratory to beach to sea boat.

CASE 5: RHYTHMIC GYMNASTICS – FROM LABORATORY TO TRAINING

Rhythmic Gymnastics (RG) is a sport in which single competitors (or five-person teams) manipulate one out of five types of apparatus: ball, clubs, hoop, ribbon, and rope. The champion is the gymnast who earns the most points, as awarded by a panel of judges, for jumping, balance, pivots, flexibility, apparatus handling, and artistic effect. In RG, the female rhythmic gymnasts perform a 90-sec routine that combines elements of gymnastic, dance, and ballet. This sport requires strength, balance, concentration, tempo, rhythm, accuracy, an artistic sense, emotional stability, coordination, self-regulation, and self-control (Blumenstein and Weinstein, 2010; Blumenstein, Yacobovitz-Balva, and Zach, 2009). RG requires the psychological skills of goal setting, self-talk, self-confidence, attention-focusing, mental relaxation, and self-awareness (Blumenstein and Weinstein, 2010; Lidor, Blumenstein, and Tenenbaum, 2007).

One year before the 2008 Beijing Olympic Games the national RG coach contacted BB and asked for his help. BB met with the coach and the athlete in his lab to understand the obstacles they were facing. The training situation was not simple due to the sport requirements, which included a heavy workload, many repetitions during the morning and evening hours, weight control, etc. In addition, the goal to achieve Olympic criterion contributed to the high tension between the athlete and her coach. BB planned his work with the athlete to be applied during lab meetings and practice sessions. In RG, during the preparation phase the focus is mainly on physical (coordination, balance, flexibility, strength) and technical practice. The gymnast spends a great deal of time on repetitions of the specific movements which comprise her routine. In this period, goal setting, self-talk, relaxation, and concentration exercises with biofeedback (BFB) were provided. The main goal was to increase motivation and self-confidence, and improve attention focusing. An example of mental session in the lab is presented below.

Sunday, 13:00-14:00 in lab

Introductory part:

- Identify the main training goals of the week

Main part:

- Concentration exercise with Galvanic Skin Response(GSR) BFB: 5-7 times x 20-30 sec.
- Imagery of competitive exercise with ball: 2-3 times with an emphasis on concentration skills and the technical aspects of performance
- Self-talk during the precompetitive routine.

Final part

- Relaxation with BFB games: "Fish" game, level 7-8.

During his visits to the practices, BB focused on improving the training atmosphere, normalizing the relationship between the coach and gymnast, and transferring mental skills from the lab to the field (e.g., concentration, self-talking). In the end of the training, the gymnast was asked to practice on imagery, while the goal was to be able to image a "clean" performance, and then relaxation (5-10 min). During the preparation phase, a "map of difficulties" for each exercise was established for the gymnast. The gymnast marked on the map the places in her exercise where she felt fearful, dangerous, or hesitant. For example, in this stage, the gymnast found 15 critical places in her exercise with the ball that caused her imagery time of this exercise to be longer compared to the ideal competitive performance time (approximately 2:15 min vs. 1:30 min). To improve her performance, BB's approach was to decrease the number of critical places that led to shorter imagery time. This was achieved by focusing during imagery mainly on the technical side of the exercise, and performing many imagery repetitions in the lab and the field.

After a few weeks, a significant improvement in the athlete's performance was observed by both the coach and the athlete. Therefore, the athlete was asked to once again sketch her routine, and to make a new map of difficulties. This time the number of critical places and performance times decreased dramatically (from 15 to 7 critical places; from approximately 2:15 min to 1:40 min). During the competitive phase, BB and the athletes continued working on imagery in the lab and during practice, and achieved approximately 1:31 min in performance, with four critical places on the third and last "map of difficulties".

Version 1: Beginning of mental practice (preparation phase)

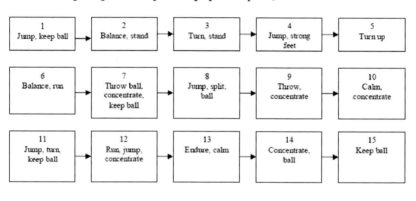

Version 2: In progress (preparation phase)

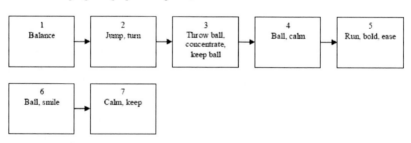

Version 3: Before competition (competitive phase)

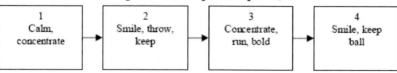

Figure 3.1. Maps of difficulties in gymnastic exercise with a ball.

During the competitive phase BB continued his work with the gymnast in the lab and in practice settings. In this phase the main objective was to improve the pre-competitive routine and to maintain high self-confidence. Following is an example of a mental session in the lab setting.

Wednesday, 13:00-14:00 (after morning training), laboratory setting

Introductory part:

- Positive thinking (good performance, self-confidence)
- Concentration exercise with GSR BFB 5-10 times x 10-20 sec

Main part:

- Imagery with GSR control (competition situation using noises by Video Camera Recorder–VCR)
- Precompetitive routine: relax-concentrate-imagery: ball exercise with GSR and time control (3 attempts)
- Relaxation: 5 min
- Precompetitive routine: relax-concentrate-imagery: ribbon exercise with GSR and time control (3 attempts)

Final part:

- Muscle relaxation: 10-15 min with music

During BB's work with the gymnast he became aware of an interesting trend. When the gymnast practiced her routine with imagery, her performance time was related to her pre-performance emotional state (measured by GSR). As can be seen below, the gymnast's emotional state was 100-120kΩ when the time of the performance was between 1:29 min-1:30 min, similar to competition demands.

Performance Time During Imagery	Emotional State Before Imagery Measured by GSR
1:29-1:30 min	100-120 kΩ
1:40-1:45 min	200-230 kΩ
2:05-2:10 min	350-400 kΩ

Table 3.1. The Gymnast's Best Results (2007-2008)

Event	Country	Year	Achievement
Olympic Games	Beijing, China	2008	9
LA Lights Invitational	United States of America	2007	3
Grand Prix Deventer	Holland	2007	5
Grand Prix Final - Rope	Israel	2007	6
Grand Prix Final - Hoop	Israel	2007	4
Grand Prix Final - Clubs	Israel	2007	4
Grand Prix Final - Ribbon	Israel	2007	4

This trend could be seen in almost all of the gymnast's routines. Out of the four exercises the gymnast practiced, improvement was faster in ribbon and ball exercises as compared to the ropes and clubs exercises. This can be explained by the gymnast's priorities and preferences. For example, she connected to the ball exercise music and enjoyed her routine more than she did for the club exercise and music background.

This approach was successfully applied by the gymnast at various top level events (Table 3.1).

In this case PST, like training in general, was also a systematic process of optimization, especially before the main competitions. The gymnast was among the best ten gymnasts in the world – a fantastic personal and country achievement.

CASE 6: WINDSURFING –TEN-MONTH COOPERATION AT SEA AS A STARTING POINT FOR A LONG-TERM RELATIONSHIP

This case study has its own uniqueness. From one aspect, it was the first attempt of mental cooperation with a windsurfer in our country. Furthermore, it was also the first time that BB provided intensive consultancy at the beach and sea. The story begins in September 1994, when one of the most famous and successful athletes in Israel called BB and asked to meet and discuss psychological issues in his sport, windsurfing. BB had no personal or professional experience in this sport. Therefore, during the first meeting the athlete explained the sport and its training and competition demands. BB told the windsurfer about his professional experience working with former Soviet athletes and his current research in psychological skills training, especially with biofeedback. The windsurfer was not aware of any concrete problems that he had, but asked BB to observe his training and to recommend some mental skills that he could acquire to improve his performance. BB readily agreed to visit the athlete's training sessions, without understanding to the "adventure" he was getting into! The next day BB came to the beach with white pants, was unsure of his expectations. The coach invited BB to his boat and they sailed for four hours in the sea, observing and guiding the windsurfer. During this time BB and the coach discussed mental obstacles in windsurfing in general, and important specific skills the athlete should acquire. After that meeting BB went to the library and searched for any publication, either popular or/and scientific, regarding windsurfing. Generally, the scientific and popular literature about windsurfing was scarce. Most of the information was connected to the technical and tactical aspects of windsurfing.

During the next meeting, BB already knew what specific questions to ask that indicated understanding, such as questions about wind, the athlete's strategies with a variety of wind directions, and different aspects of his physical, technical and tactical preparations. BB began to understand that from the psychological aspect, the athlete had to face hard training conditions such as volume (many hours in the sea and in the fitness hall), loneliness, adverse weather conditions, monotonous training, and finally difficulties in measuring progress. Based on all the above, BB recommended the ways he could contribute to athlete's success. Relaxation during the race for optimal performance and after training for recovery purposes; development of a pre-competitive routine before the competition and start; optimization of behavior between races; self-regulation and concentration before the start. Based on these observations, BB recommended a model for psychological skills training, starting with learning psychological skills in the laboratory and transferring them to the actual setting of training and competition (Blumenstein and Orbach, 2011, in press).

We would like to discuss three basic psychological skills that the athlete transferred from the laboratory to the sea. The first one was muscle relaxation, which we trained in the laboratory with electromyography (EMG) BFB. In the lab the athlete learned relatively easily how to achieve muscle relaxation. For example, the athlete succeeded in achieving muscle relaxation quickly and accurately using EMG of the frontalis muscle, which was between the limits of 2.4–2.6 to 0.6-0.8 during 10-15 sec. The next step was practicing the relaxation skills with exercises that imitate actual training, such as relaxing either side of the body, as the surfer should do during the planning and the pumping parts of surfing. The surfer admitted that these relaxation skills assisted him in performing better and more easily. After a short time the surfer was able to transfer these skills to practice and eventually to competitions.

Another psychological skill that was transferred from the lab to the sea was concentration. The athlete trained on concentration in the lab with GSR BFB (Blumenstein and Orbach, 2011, in press). Based on this, he trained on imagery with exercises, such as 1-minute before the start and specific concentration in the last 10-seconds before the start. As indicated before, the surfer applied these skills during competition races.

Lastly, we developed the athlete's behavioral patterns between races on the beach during waiting regimes. Specifically, we focused on what the athlete concentrates and thinks about, and what music he should listen to, etc. Most of this work was done on the beach and in the sea boat while using portable BFB devices. The practice was very demanding, due to the setting and the length of the training sessions.

The beauty of this relationship was the mutual cooperation between BB and the athlete. BB helped the athlete to achieve optimal performance and on the other hand, the athlete helped BB, who had recently immigrated to the country, to better understand the culture, history, tradition, and style sports in Israel. This cooperation lasted four years; BB was part of the windsurfing team and took part in numerous training camps and successful competitions. During this period the athlete achieved silver medals in the World Championships (1992, 1997, and 1998), and was European Champion (1993 and 1997). He ranked number one in the general world ranking number in 1992, 1997, and 1998.

CASE 7: SWIMMING – FROM LABORATORY TO NATIONAL CHAMPIONSHIP

This case study tells the story of a 16-years old swimmer, specializing in the 50m and 100m breaststroke. Initially, when the swimmer approached BB in November 2010, his personal records in 50 m was 29.30 sec and in 100 m 1:04:57 sec. The main reason for approaching BB was that he had made no progress in his results for more than a year, and the coach believed that the core of the problem was the mental aspect. The coach recommended that the athlete to approach BB. The athlete arrived at the first meeting with his father. The swimmer had to deal with a few typical mistakes that young athletes are inclined to make. The athlete was oriented only on outcome/results goals. During training swimmers are requested to perform intervals where the focus is on time-demands. Therefore, the focus of the swimmer usually was on the time, and especially under the stressful conditions of competition. To resolve this, BB recommended staying in focus in each training session only on the technical aspects of the chosen exercise. In addition, the swimmer exhibited bad competition behavior. He would sit in the crowd and observe all his friends' heats; this led him to be tense and unstable emotionally. When his turn arrived, the swimmer felt emotionally drained and his muscles were tensed and "close". Therefore, we planned to change his competition behavior and to establish an optimal pre-competitive routine. The major goal of the swimmer was to break his personal best during the winter National Championship in February 2011. This meant that we had a time span of five months to prepare the swimmer.

Table 3.2. Example of the Swimmer's Weekly PST (first month)

	Days of the week						
	Sun.	Mon.	Tue.	Wed.	Thu.	Fri.	Sat.
Relaxation 10-15 min			H*			H	
Relaxation 1-5 min	T*						
Relaxation 10, 20, 30 sec.		L*			L		
Imagery: 5x50m (performance goal)		L			L		
Imagery: 5x100m (performance goal)		L			L		
Attention-focusing exercises with GSR/BFB: 10x10 sec		L			L		
Self-talk	T		T			T	
Pre-competitive routine						T	
Tempo/rhythm exercise		L			L		

T* = Training setting; L* = Laboratory setting; H* = Home exercise

Due to the time constraints, we used a short version of the W5SA, in which we focused on specific skills that are important for the swimmer. In the first month we started with two meetings per week during which we focused on techniques such as muscle relaxation and relaxation incorporating BFB (Blumenstein and Bar-Eli, 2001), imagery (Hall, 2001), and self-talk (Henschen, 2005). The psychological techniques were introduced to the swimmer in three different frameworks: (1) laboratory setting, (2) training (practice sessions), and (3) home settings. The use of the psychological techniques administered to the swimmer in this (and the following) month had two main objectives: first of all, to provide the swimmer with the fundamentals of relaxation, imagery, self-talk, and BFB, so he could use these techniques while acquiring and refining a variety of technical skills; and second, to develop a pre-competitive routine, so he could use it before competitions. Table 3.2 presents various examples of the use of psychological techniques during this period.

At the end of this month the swimmer had to take part in a local swimming competition. During a mental training before the competition, the swimmer performed five trials of time-measured 100 m using imagery. The goal was to concentrate on the technical aspects in each heat, while changing the line imaged in every trial. The swimmer achieved the following results:

5 x 100 m: 46.18 sec, 52.15 sec, 56.2 sec, 1:03:37 sec, 1:05:58 sec.

The swimmer's time for the imagery was not consistent. He had difficulty concentrating on the technical aspect, and his imagery perspective was either internal or external. In spite of the inconsistency, the swimmer was aware of the importance of focusing on performance goals (vs. outcome goal) and muscle relaxation, before and during performance. This led the swimmer to be more self-confident, and he developed a pre-competitive routine. During the competition the swimmer achieved a personal record of 1:04:47! As a side note, it is important to know that the swimmer used simple psychological knowledge acquired from his work with BB, which helped him to achieve a personal record. Therefore, the swimmer's readiness to continue with the psychological work was positive. In the following two months the focus was on muscle relaxation, goal setting, performance goals, a precompetitive routine, and concentration before the heat. Example of a mental session two weeks before the winter national championship is below:

Monday, 13:00-14:00, Wingate Institute, January 2011:
Introduction part:

- Analyzing weekly goals and athlete's current psychophysiological states.
- Concentration exercise: 10-15 sec x 10 times with GSR BFB control.

Main part:

- Muscle relaxation: 10 sec x 5; 20 sec x 5; 30 sec x 5.
- Imagery (concentrate on performance goals): 50 m x 5 and 100 m x 5 with time measure.
- Pre-competitive routine: Warm-up (focus on performance goals), waiting before heat (relaxation and concentration internally), start (relaxation and concentration on line), performance (focus on technical aspects and turns).

Final part:

- Relaxation with music 10 min.

During the last meeting on before the national championship competition the swimmer practiced his imagery skills, attempting to simulate the competitive heats of 50 m and 100 m. To achieve that, the imagery was practiced while using competitive noises. The results were:

- 50 m: 29.16 sec, 29.10 sec.
- 100 m: 1:04:19 min, 1:04:02 min, and in the final 1:03:79 min.

On 18.2.11 the swimmer took part in the winter National Championship, which included preliminary and final heats. His achievements are as follows:

- 50 m: preliminary 29:07 sec (personal best); final 28:95 sec (personal best).
- 100 m: Preliminary 1:04:30 min (personal best); Final 1:03:70 min (personal best).

The swimmer and his parents were very satisfied with the swimmer's achievements, and thus decided to continue the mental support with BB in preparation for the summer National Championship.

CASE 8: POLE VAULT – FROM LABORATORY TO EUROPEAN CHAMPIONSHIP

Pole vault is one of the most technical events in of track and field. Pole vault athletes must be multitalented athletes; they are usually talented sprinters (10.4-10.7 sec in 100m run), jumpers (more than 2m high jump and 7.5meters long jump), hurdlers (13.7-14.4sec in 110m run), and they have to be good acrobats and gymnasts. They have a high level coordination, flexibility, and power strength. Pole vaulters are bold with a high level of concentration, self-regulation skills, and patience. Competitions can last for 4-5 hours. During the approach the pole vaulter sprints down the runway in a rhythmic, relaxed style so as to achieve maximum speed (9.2-9.4 m/sec) and this correct position to initiate takeoff at the end of the approach. Elite pole vaulters use approaches with 18-22 strides (35-45m). In competition, the athlete has to choose a starting height and has three attempts to clear it. Often the decision regarding the height he/she chooses to jump can prove crucial for taking the victory.

Technical and physical preparations are important components of the athletes' training. Moreover, in physical preparation the athletes practice on applying power very fast, control of the body and "cooperation" between muscle efforts and the pole. Psychological preparation in pole vault focuses on developing concentration, self-confidence, thought-control, and visualization (Blumenstein and Weinstein, 2010; Dosil, 2006). Moreover, an important component of psychological preparation is establishing a fast and stable routine before the attempt, and an ability to identify and focus on the "right" moment to jump considering external and internal factors (e.g., wind direction and intensity, noise, self-readiness), and only then to begin the approach.

This case presents a few short systematical psychological services with an experienced and famous pole vaulter during a long time period. Our work with pole vaulter "A" was based on the periodization principle, but mostly on his vast experience. "A" came to pole vaulting from the decathlon, and when we started our mutual work in 2003 he was already a famous athlete achieving one silver and one bronze medal in the World Championship (Spain 1999, Canada 2001) and two gold medals in the European Championship (Belgium 2000, Germany, 2002). However, the athlete heard about BB's work and during a lecture for elite athletes, "A" approached BB and asked that they cooperate starting from the next season. In the past BB was a sprinter and therefore he understood track and field's language and demands. This led to a faster and full cooperation with the mental intervention. After two weeks of visiting the athlete's training, BB proposed several potential points for improving the athlete's pre-performance routine, especially working on concentration and imagery. Most of their work was conducted during practice (stadium and gym). The athlete continued to use this model of behavior and cooperation with the sport psychology consultants for several seasons.

In the preparation phase, which lasted approximately three months, BB and the "A" worked systematically – one meeting in the lab and two or three meetings in the field. In the lab meetings we focused on improving:

- Relaxation abilities using EMG/GSR BFB control;
- Imagery skills with special attention on the technical side of the take off and the flight phase;
- Fast and stable concentration skills;
- Pre-performance routine.

In this case the pre-performance routine included the following components: Create the optimal state of full readiness for initiating the attempt – mentally imagery of start – run – 2-3 last strides including plant position and take-off. During practice we worked on strengthening his mental skills by so that he could transfer them from the lab to real-life conditions. Special attention was given to concentration time before the athlete began his run. We measured this parameter in the lab using imagery, in training attempts and in competition. When the time was approximately the same throughout the above conditions, it was possible to claim that the athlete was ready to perform successfully. As can be seen in Table 3.3, the concentration time during successful competition attempts was slightly shorter compared to imagery attempts in the laboratory In addition, when the height of the bar increased, the concentration time increased as well (Table 3.3).

Table 3.3. Concentration Time on Start

Location / Height	5.40m-5.60m	5.65m-5.80m
Laboratory	14-17 sec	16-20 sec
Field	12-16 sec	14-18 sec
Competition	11-14 sec	12-15 sec

Two examples of lab and field meetings are presented below:
Laboratory meeting:
Monday, 12:00-13:00, Wingate Institute
Preparation part:

- Analysis of weekly and daily performance goals

Main part:

- Fast concentration by command with GSR BFB control: 10-20sec x 10-15 times
- Imagery: Jump of starting height (5.40-5.45m) while focusing on easy, rhythm run, boldly take off, and an exact flight phase: 4-5 times

Final part:

- Relaxation 10-15 min.

In the field meeting, the psychological techniques were modified according to training demands and the concrete situation.
Field meeting (evening training at the stadium):
Concentration exercises:

- After warm-up 10-15 sec x 2-3 times
- Before jump   10-15 sec x 1 time

Imagery:

- Between jumps; focus on technical aspects

Relaxation:

- After training 10-15 min with emphasis on positive points in practice.

During the competitive phase we cooperated with our biomechanics lab staff from the Zinman College to analyze the pole vaulter's technique. This information had a positive effect on the imagery, enabling it to be more clear and vivid. It should be noted that collaboration with other scientific sport disciplines (e.g., nutrition, physiology) can significantly improve the professional level of the training process. The core of our mental training during the competitive phase was improving the athlete's precompetitive routine for the European Championship in Gothenburg, Sweden (2006). Special attention was given to relaxation between attempts, behavior between attempts, and mini warm-ups before attempts. For example, we discussed with the athlete his behavior in possible situations such as when the athlete has to wait a long time for his turn. We developed a behavioral plan for this situation that included reading the sport news of an Israeli newspaper which he prepared in advance, taking a short walk, and sitting on the side with his back to the bar. During the competition the athlete won with only two successful attempts (5.50m and 5.70m). He had to wait for more than one hour between the attempts, and therefore he had to apply our mental routine. The athlete acknowledged that his routine had a negative effect on his opponents, and helped him to reach his peak performance on his way to achieving the gold medal.

CASE 9: KAYAKING (K1-1000) – FROM LABORATORY TO OLYMPIC FINAL

Kayaking is a sport discipline that requires high endurance and speed, an explosive start, and the maintenance of high speed and tempo throughout the entire distance of the race (Blumenstein and Lidor, 2004; Ford, 1995; Lidor, Blumenstein, and Tenenbaum, 2007). The psychological skills required for peak performance in kayaking are focusing, relaxation, mental control, self-regulation, and mental toughness (Blumenstein and Bar-Eli, 2001; Lidor et al., 2007). In our case we present an athlete who specialized in flatwater races across a 500m and 1000m course. His strong event was the 1000m race (K1-1000), in which his best achievement before cooperation with the sport psychologist was finals "B", sixteenth place in international competitions.

In 2001, after the World Cup, the elite sport department approached BB and asked him to begin work with the athlete, with the main goal of preparing the athlete for the 2004 Olympic Games in Athens. Our work with the athlete was based on a previous model, which included systematic work during the preparation phase and intensive work in the competitive phase. In the preparation phase the kayaker was involved in difficult and monotonous work, such as weight-lifting, interval running training, and distance running. In addition, during this period the kayakers focus on improving their individual style of paddling, developing strategies and race plans, and creating optimal tempo-rhythm while paddling (Lidor et al., 2007). The psychological training was provided in the lab (once a week) and on the river (twice a week). In order for the kayaker to achieve progress during the preparation phase, the mental techniques that he had to learn in the lab were muscle relaxation, relaxation incorporated biofeedback, imagery, and self-talk (Blumenstein and Lidor, 2004). There were two main objectives for using these psychological techniques: first, to provide the kayakers with the fundamentals of imagery, relaxation-incorporated EMG/GSR biofeedback, and self-talk, so that they could use these techniques while acquiring and refining a variety of technical skills practiced during the preparation phase; and second, to teach them the fundamentals of a relaxation technique so they could use it to recover from practice sessions and workouts at early stages of the season. Training in the river had a different flavor when psychological skills were transferred from laboratory to real life settings. During one morning practice BB was sitting with the coach in the training boat providing psychological guidance to the athlete, such as points for concentration, muscle relaxation, positive self-talk, and motivation. At the end of the practice, BB guided the athlete in relaxation with portable EMG/GSR BFB for recovery purposes.

In the competitive phase, while the volume of training was lower and the intensity increased, we focused on practice under training-simulated conditions that reflected actual competition settings. In these practices we focus on developing a race strategy or a plan with the objective of learning how to allocate the athlete's energy across the race distance. Therefore, special attention was given to actual environmental and situational factors, such as the start of the race, the distance of the race, and the finish of the race (Blumenstein and Lidor, 2004). In addition, the kayaker was taught how to perform under different weather conditions. The objective of the psychological support given to the kayaker during the competition phase was to assist him in handling pressure and coping with stress. In addition, the kayaker spent a considerable amount of time on improving his ability to maintain a high level of attention-focusing during competition, for example he developed a race plan while using an imagery technique and memorized it vividly and effectively. In addition, during the actual race, the kayaker was told to apply both attention focusing and self-talk techniques in order to appropriately execute the plan of the race. Moreover, his pre-competitive routine was developed and practiced. Examples of mental session in the laboratory and field in the competitive phase are presented below.

Laboratory meeting:
Sunday, 13:00-14:00, Wingate Institute
Preparation part:

- Analysis of weekly and daily performance goals
- Achievement motivation for successful performance in competition

Main part:

- Relaxation for 1-3 min with EMG/GSR BFB
- Imagery:
  - Start of race 5-6 times
  - Start of race with external command 3-4 times
  - Tempo/rhythm exercises 4-5 times

Final part:

- Relaxation 10-15 min.

During the field meeting, psychological techniques were applied in the kayak and were adapted to actual practice and situation.
Field meeting (morning training at the river):
Monday, 7:00-9:00, Yarkon River

- Concentration exercise:
  - After warm up of dry training 10-15 sec x 2-3 times.
  - In the kayak 10-15 sec x 2-3 times

Relaxation:

- Between 5 intervals of 250-500 m relaxation for 1 min

Self-talk:

- Using key words such as "relax" and "concentrate" during performance

Table 3.4. Athlete's Achievements
with and without Psychological Support

No Psychological Support	Psychological Support			No Psychological Support	
2001 Word Cup	2002 World Championship	2003 World Championship	2004 Olympic Games	2005	2006 World Cup
Final B Place 16	Final A Place 4	Final A Place 8	Final A Place 9	-	Final B 16

Relaxation:

- After training on the beach 10-15 min with emphasis on positive points in practice.

A similar model was applied in the next three years during our work with the athlete. The athlete significantly improved his performance and his major achievements are presented in Table 3.4 below.

The athlete's achievements during the years 2002-2004 were significantly better compared to his previous performance. The psychological support was an additional tool to the regular training, and helped the athlete to realize his full potential, as well as to establish a more consistent and better performance during competitions. After that the athlete did not achieve any significant results which were similar to the years of 2002-2004.

CONCLUSION

In this chapter we focused on five cases from individual sports. Several principals of the psychological consulting model were similar in all of them:

- Intensive and systematic psychological work with athletes in the precompetitive phase, which included laboratory and field sessions. In the competitive phase the majority of the sessions were conducted in the field.
- Establish and modify mental techniques and programs according to each sport's specific demands.

- The sport consultant is required to understand the theory and methodology of sport training while taking part in trainings and competitions.
- Integration of mental sessions in the training process as based on the periodization principle.
- Emphasis on full cooperation with the coach and participation in the training process as the coach's helper.

REFERENCES

Blumenstein, B., and Bar-Eli M. (2001). A five-step approach for biofeedback in sport. *Sportwissenschaft, 4*, 412-424.

Blumenstein, B., and Lidor, R. (2004). Psychological preparation in elite canoeing and kayaking sport programs: Periodization and planning. *Applied Research in Coaching and Athletics Annual, 19*, 24-34.

Blumenstein, B., and Orbach, I. (2011, in press). Biofeedback training in the sea. In A. Edmonds and G. Tenenbaum (Eds.), Case studies in applied psychophysiology: Neurofeedback and biofeedback treatments for advanced in human performance. Chichester, Sussex: Wiley-Blackwell.

Blumenstein, B., and Weinstein, Y. (2010) *Psychological Skills Training: Application to Elite Sport Performance.* Grand Rapids, MI: Ultimate Athlete Concepts.

Blumenstein, B., Yacobovitz-Balva, Y., and Zach, S. (2009). Psychological methods of performance enhancement in modern rhythmic gymnastics. *Leistungssport, 5*, 44-47.

Dosil, J. (2006). The psychology of athletics. In J. Dosil (Ed.), *The sport psychologist's handbook: A guide for sport-specific performance enhancement* (pp. 265-284). Chichester, UK: John Wiley and Sons, Ltd.

Ford, K. (1995). *Whitewater and sea kayaking*. Champaign, IL: Human Kinetics.

Hall, C. R. (2001). Imagery in sport and exercise. In R. Singer, H. Hausenblas, and C. Janelle (Eds.). *Handbook of sport psychology* (2nd ed., pp. 529-549). New York: Wiley.

Henschen, K. (2005). Mental practice – skill oriented. In D. Hackfort, J. Duda, and R. Lidor (Eds.). *Handbook of research in applied sport and exercise psychology: International perspectives* (pp. 19-36). Morgantown, WV: Fitness Information Technology.

Lidor, R., Blumenstein, B., and Tenenbaum, G. (2007). Periodization and planning of psychological preparation in individual and team sports. In B. Blumenstein, R. Lidor, and G. Tenenbaum (Eds.). *Psychology of sport training* (pp. 137-161). Oxford, UK: Meyer and Meyer Sport.

Chapter 4

PSYCHOLOGICAL SKILLS TRAINING IN TEAM SPORTS

ABSTRACT

Chapter 4 focuses on three case studies from team sports: Two from soccer and one from basketball. Three models of psychological service with professional soccer teams and with a youth basketball team from a sport academy are presented. All the case studies are based on long-term cooperation between the coaching staff, team players, and sport psychology consultant. Although the focus is on team sports, the psychological skills training (PST) is provided in both an individual and team manner. In addition, the authors suggest the use of psychological strategies and behavioral models which can be used effectively by the coach as well as by teammates.

INTRODUCTION

Soccer is the world's most popular game, in which players attempt to create goal-scoring opportunities through individual control of the ball, such as by dribbling, passing the ball to a teammate, and taking shots at the goal which is guarded by the opposing goalkeeper. Opposing players may try to regain control of the ball by intercepting a pass or tackling the opponent in possession of the ball. In soccer important psychological skills are required, such as concentration, self-regulation, self-talk, and positive thinking (Dosil, 2006; Lidor, Blumenstein, and Tenenbaum, 2007). *Basketball* is a game in which five players perform against five opposing players in a rapid and changeable environment (Wooden, 1980). Basketball players are required to spend a great deal of time on improving physical abilities such as agility, speed, explosive power, and strength. Moreover, technical, tactical, and psychological preparations are important components of the daily training program in basketball (Burke, 2006; Henschen and Cook, 2003; Lidor et al., 2007). Two cases from soccer and one case from basketball are presented below.

CASE 10: PROFESSIONAL SOCCER CLUB – FROM TRAINING CAMP TO NATIONAL LEAGUE CHAMPIONSHIP

In this case we will discuss our approach to working with a professional soccer team (males, mean age=24.8) from Division 1, which is the highest professional football division in country. In the past BB worked with different soccer teams and collaborated with their coaches, therefore it was not a surprise a well-known coach approached BB and invited him to work with his new team. The first meeting with the coach was in coffee shop located away from the media and team fans. The coach informed BB about the team's current situation. His urgent need was to "build a new team while there is a lot of tension and stress from the media, fans, and club management". Therefore, the team administration and coaching staff decided to complete the preparation phase toward the new season at a one-month training camp in Holland. The next meeting was in BB's laboratory, where the coach was introduced to various psychological techniques such as relaxation, concentration, biofeedback (BFB) training, imagery, etc. During the meeting, the coach presented the player's stories and attempted to determine if these techniques could be tailored to the athlete's needs. The coach asked BB "are you ready to take on the challenge?" Before giving his final consent BB met with key people in the team, such as the head manager, the coaching staff, the sport medicine staff, and some of the player, in order to collect more information about the team's condition. BB learned that everyone shared the same goal – "team success"; however, the road to achieve it was not clear. A few of the problems that the team faced were double function in some of the major positions and ambiguous expectations from several officials. This was not part of BB's domain, but there was no doubt they were affecting the team's atmosphere. In regard to the players, BB realized that the younger players had a great deal of motivation to succeed and improve. On the other hand, the motivation of the veterans was affected by their unclear future position within the "new" team. After collecting the information and discussing the situation with the coach, BB decided to accept the challenge.

Before leaving for Holland, the head coach allocated responsibilities to each of the staff, including the sport psychology consultant. Two models of psychological service were developed:

1. *Basic Model:* Focus on 5-6 young players with high potential and work with the other players according to the coach's request or the situation. In addition, provide educational work with the team, including lectures and consultation to the coaching staff. The underlying goal was to develop team cohesion by improving players' mental skills and their accountability to the team. An ideal outcome of this approach was the mentoring of young players by the veteran players.
2. *Possible Model:* Work separately with three groups: Young, veteran, and star (foreign) players, and provide psychological support to coaches.

BB preferred the Basic plan and the next day BB and the team left for Holland. The delegation included 25 players (22 Israelis and three foreigners), three coaches, a team doctor, two physiotherapists, one official, and BB himself. The location of the training camp was optimal for training and included all the necessary facilities, such as two soccer fields, a fitness hall, a swimming pool, a sauna, a small dining room, and very comfortable living conditions.

The coaches and BB joined the players in a light morning jog in the forest. The players liked this interaction with the staff. In the evening a team meeting was held, and after the coach's talk the group discussed psychological preparation in soccer. BB explained some of the psychological skills needed for successful performance in soccer and the psychological techniques that could be employed, including a demonstration of BFB for developing those skills. The players had many questions about pre-competitive routines, concentration during the game, and fast comebacks after mistakes. BB gave the players some solutions to the issues they raised. On that first evening, the head coach and BB finalized the Basic program as the model to be used by the sport psychologist while working with the players, coach, and medical staff during the training camp (see Figure 4.1).

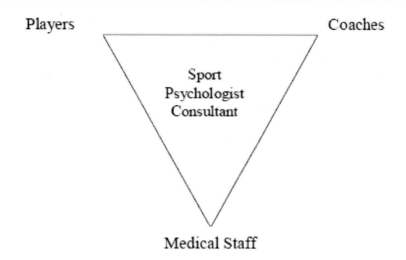

Figure 4.1. Model of psychological service with professional soccer team during training camp.

The coach proposed that BB work with six players: five young players and one foreigner. Each of them had to work on different parameters, such as unstable concentration and emotional state for the young players and low self-regulation for the foreigner. BB at first had meetings with individual players, and later worked with two of them together. The meetings took place 3-4 times a week; each meeting lasted about 30 min. In the individual meetings, psychological techniques such as relaxation (Henschen, 2005), imagery (Hall, 2001), attention focusing (Moran, 2003; 2005), self-talk (Henschen, 2005) and biofeedback (BFB) training (Blumenstein and Bar-Eli, 2005; Blumenstein, Bar-Eli, and Collins, 2002) were addressed.

A few days after the beginning of the training camp, the players approached the coach and asked for several lectures by BB on the topic of mental training in soccer. The focus of the first meeting was on the various mental techniques in sport which could be used by the players. In Table 4.1 we summarize players' responses in regard to the favorite mental techniques used by them before, during, and after the game.

Some of the conclusions from the meetings and from the above table were that most of the players were not aware of what self-regulation in a game is, or how to use muscle relaxation during or after a game. The most commonly-used techniques by the players before and during the game were self-talk, positive thinking, and concentration. Based on the above, BB applied techniques such as relaxation, effective self-talk, and positive thinking.

Table 4.1. Mental Techniques Applied by the Soccer Players (n = 25)

Mental Skills	Before Game	During Game	After Game
Relaxation	4 (16%)	2 (8%)	6 (24%)
Concentration	10 (40%)	9 (36%)	2 (8%)
Self-Talk	12 (48%)	16 (64%)	4 (16%)
Positive Thinking	8 (32%)	14 (56%)	6 (24%)
Imagery	6 (24%)	-	4 (16%)
Music	4 (16%)	-	10 (40%)
Pre-Performance Routine	12 (48%)	-	-
Goal Setting	4 (16%)	2 (8%)	1 (4%)
Self-Regulation	2 (8%)	3 (12%)	2 (8%)

In the subsequent team meetings, BB discussed their questions "how should I prepare for the game?" and "what is the best way for me to prepare to the game?". After this lecture, the coach asked BB for three team relaxation sessions per week for 20 minutes each, at the end of the evening practice. In addition, the three foreign players approached BB and asked to learn how to use BFB to improve concentration. It is important to note that BB had the full cooperation of the coaching staff, who believed that the mental program was having a positive effect on the players' skills and on group cohesion.

The team-building process usually includes four stages: Forming, storming, norming, and performing (Tuckman, 1965; Tuckman and Jensen, 1977). In this case study the storming stage, which involves conflicts between the team members, was relatively short and smooth. This was probably due to the intensive training and constant presence of the sport psychologist, who was able to sort things out and make immediate decisions. Therefore, during most of this training period the team members were in the norming and performing stages. In addition to training, the players had a few hours of free time in which they either stayed in their rooms listening to music or played snooker in the hotel. The delegation also visited historical sites in the town a few times.

At the end of the first week, the team played a friendly game with a local soccer team. It was holiday time, and many people were in the park, there was music in the street, and overall an optimistic and positive atmosphere could be felt. The coach let the young players begin the first half, while in the second half the more experienced players continued the game. The score in the first half was 0:0 and at the end of the game we were at an advantage of 2:0. The team members were in a good mood and had high motivation. In the evening the coach met with the players and analyzed the game. He noted that in this game the players had lost many balls due to inaccurate passes. In addition to emotional issues, the game's organization and the communication between players were poor. For example, game statistics indicated the following results: Passing the ball with one accurate pass (37%), with two accurate passes (28%), and three or more accurate passes (17%).

In the next week, in addition to the training routine, the focus was on players' communication, sportsmanship, anticipation, and relaxation during the game. On the following Saturday the team played against a local team from the 2nd Holland League. The game was started with the base team and on the 25th minute one of our players scored a goal, which turned out to be the final result. In the game analysis the coach focused on higher level strategy, such as better tactical and game organization (two accurate passes were 36% and three or more were 45%). Overall, the players showed improvement in their communication and sportsmanship skills. However, when analyzing the game, the coach commented on the fact that the team demonstrated a bad final part of the game (e.g., they kept the score safe for the last 10 min).

The focus of the last week was on team cohesion, while one of the main goals was including the foreigner players to be part of the team (one each from Bulgaria, Ukraine, and Georgia). The coach, with the assistance of BB, organized a wonderful evening which included good Georgian national food, Bulgarian dancing, and Ukrainian songs. The next day the team played against a Dutch soccer team from the first division. The game was interesting. Although the score in the first half was 1:0, the final score was 1:1, which was a good indication of the mental and physical toughness of the team. Players were tired at the end of the game but very satisfied with their performance. The overall team feeling was that "We have a team", and that they were going back home with a lot of optimism and motivation to continue and improve.

According to the coach's request, BB continued to work individually with 4-5 players and the overall team for the next three months. In this period a weekly psychological consultancy schedule was provided, according to the official Saturday game in the national league.

The day after the game, a short team session was provided which included congratulatory remarks and support based on individual performances in the game; the players were sensitive to BB's remarks about their performance. This was followed by muscle relaxation for 10-15 minutes.

– On *Mondays and Tuesdays*: Individual sessions in which BB worked on specific psychological issues with 2-3 players.

  - On *Wednesdays*: Individual sessions in which BB worked basically on the players' self-confidence
  - On *Thursdays*: Team sessions on motivation, pre-competitive routines, team cohesion, and/or team communication.
  - On *Fridays*: According to coaches request individual or team sessions were provided, based on the team current state or on specific situations, with selected players chosen by the coach.

During this period the team was placed fourth or fifth in the national premier league. However, the absence of professional team management and bad organization were the chief stress factors in this period. After three months BB finished his work with team, with good memories and relationships with the coach and players. In the future, most of them had further cooperation with BB in Israel and Europe.

In general, it can be said that intensive and systematic work with a soccer team in a training camp is a good start for a sport psychologist consultant. Full cooperation with the coaching staff is a main factor for work success. In our case, the main difficulty was a conservative team management and organization.

CASE 11: YOUTH SOCCER TEAM: TEN MONTHS OF COOPERATION WITH THE TEAM

This case study is about a youth soccer department from one of the favorite soccer clubs in the country. The chief manager of the club approached BB and asked for his cooperation with the coaches and young players (age 15-17). The club was more than a training place for the players. The players arrived at the club after school and stayed there until the evening. The club had ideal training and social conditions for youth players. Before and after training the players spent time in the game room, after soccer practice they were given supper, and after a short rest they did their homework with the help of a few students, especially in English and Math. The surroundings were very organized, clean, and friendly.

BB, together with the coach, developed a joint work plan for 10 months (from October until July 2005), which included weekly individual and team meetings, monthly meeting with the coaching staff, and a meeting with the parents every two months.

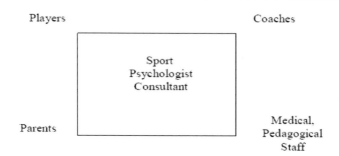

Figure 4.2. Model of psychological services with a youth soccer team during a 10-month season.

The coach recommended seven talented soccer players to BB for individual meetings. They discussed their personal qualities, sport history, and coach's expectations regarding future achievements.

In the *first* month BB met with the chosen players six times, with the focus learning fundamental mental techniques such as relaxation, imagery, concentration, and BFB training (a short version of the Wingate Five-Step Approach–W5SA). The first monthly meeting with the coaching staff concerned topics regarding the psychology of a youth soccer team, such as group dynamics. In addition, during the meeting questions were raised regarding daily situations that the staff encountered. Most of the questions concerned relationships, communication, and pressure from the parents. As a consequence, BB recommended that routine meetings be held with the parents, in which topics would be discussed such as having a soccer player in family – the support and limitations. The pedagogical staff who advised the players on educational material attended these lectures as well. In addition to the lecture, BB answered personal questions from the parents. The first month was very successful.

In the *second* month the learning process was continued by having six individual meetings per each chosen player, with the addition of positive or negative verbal remarks. In addition, the group meeting for the coaching staff included topics such as leaders in the soccer team, and the relationship between the coach and players as leaders.

After BB attended two official games and discussed his observations with the coach, he then concluded that the team would benefit from monthly team meetings, with the first one having the topics of psychological preparation for games and communication in games. In addition, short meetings with the pedagogical staff were provided in which communication and cooperation with players throughout the season was discussed.

During the *third* month the focus of the meetings was on topics that related to specific preparation for the games. During the six individual meetings in which the main emphasize was on simulation, BB worked with the players on issues such as performance relaxation, pre-competitive routine, self-talk, and stress distractions (using audio/visual fragments from Video Camera Recorder–VCR). The main topic of the meeting with the coaching staff was on management during the soccer game. Lastly, the meeting with the parents involved ways to support the players, and which tips to provide them with at home before a game.

The goal of the *fourth* month was the application of mental techniques in training and competition. The format was somewhat different than that of the previous month. Instead of six individual meetings per each chosen player, four individual and two team meetings were conducted. Moreover, some of the individual meetings were conducted with a partner in a competitive environment, such as concentration exercises with portable Galvanic Skin Response (GSR) BFB (*Mind* and *Stress* Master by Atlas Ltd), which measures self-regulation skill. In addition, BB attended two games and two practice sessions. After one of the practices BB provided team relaxation sessions, and after the second meeting BB talked about imagery before a game. The meeting with the coaching staff was on how to maintain optimal motivation before the game.

During the *fifth* month BB continued to work with the players on the application of mental techniques specific to training and competition settings. More specifically, they worked on pre-competitive routines, self-talk during the game, and relaxation after training and games. During that month BB attended one game. During the meeting with the coach, BB taught him how and when to incorporate the mental techniques into their practice routine. For example, BB explained to the coaching staff how imagery can affect technical preparation or self-regulation, concentration before game, relaxation after training, etc. In the parents' meeting they received instructions in regard to the recommended sport regimes the players should follow. In addition, BB met with the team doctor to receive updates on the physical and recovery conditions some of the players may experience.

The main goal of the next two months, the *sixth* and *seventh*, was an intensive application of the mental techniques during practice and games, in order for the players to be prepared for each competitive situation. BB met three times with each chosen player, and had a team discussion twice during each month. Special focus was given to concentration skills before practice, muscle relaxation after training, and team motivation. The discussion with the coach was based on a model of psychological support during a one-week training period which included muscle relaxation after game, weekly goals, motivation, and pre-competitive routines before upcoming games.

During the *eight* and *ninth* months, BB spent time with the players, especially during team practice and official games. BB visited four training sessions and three games. The main important parameters for that period were pre-competition routine, optimal excitation level before the game and self-talk and communication in the game. The talk with the coaching staff was on current team leaders and ways to communicate with them. The presentation for the parents focused on psychological factors and behavior of the players two days before a game.

The *tenth* and last month was critical for the coaching staff, since they were preparing for two final games, one home and one away, against major and strong opponents. The focus was on effective communication and team cohesion as part of the preparation for the games. Moreover, there was personal work with the team captain about his support for players before and during game. BB met with the coaching staff to optimize the pre-competitive excitation stages. BB visited four practices and two games. The final score was 1:1 for the away game and 2:1 for the home game.

To summarize this case, we want to call attention to the full cooperation between the coach's staff and the sport psychology consultant, the combination individual mental trainings and team work, to enable the transfer from "room" meetings to "real life" practice. The head team manager admitted that the past season had been the best season for the youth department. The team achieved first place in the National Championship, and four players (18 years or older) were invited to play in the next season in senior soccer clubs. After three seasons two of them played in our national soccer team. In addition to the objective achievements such as place in the league, the coach testified that the cohesion and the atmosphere on the team had improved and become more professional.

CASE 12: BASKETBALL TEAM – A LONG-TERM MULTIDISCIPLINARY COOPERATION

In this case we will describe our experience with a youth basketball team from a "Sport Academy" – The Center for the Development of Sport Giftedness. The academy was established at the Wingate Institute in 1990. Its

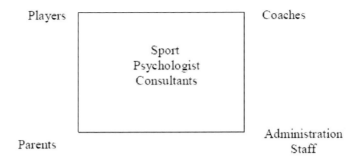

Figure 4.3. Model of professional multi-disciplinary cooperation with a youth basketball team.

main goal is developing to the maximum the potential of young talented athletes. The sport-gifted youth are selected on merit and are trained by top-level coaches. They are under constant medical and mental supervision provided by the Ribstein center for Sport Medicine Sciences and Research. The young athletes live at the Wingate Institute, study together at a nearby school, and train intensively. Most of them represent the country at international competitions, where they have attained extremely creditable results.

The academy administration initiated a meeting with the sport psychologist consultants (B.B. and I.O.) in which the logistic aspects and the model of cooperation were discussed (see Figure 4.3).

As can be seen in the figure 4.3, there was cooperation between the sport psychologist consultants and the following groups:

Sport psychology consultants – Administration staff: Initially, there was a meeting with the academy director and a social worker, in which the system and structure of the academy was explained. The goals, expectations, and potential possibilities for psychological service for the basketball team were discussed. In addition, the structure of daily work with the players, such as appointments and reports, were established. The general rule was that a player would approach the social worker to ask for an appointment with the psychology staff. Then the social worker would get in touch with the mental consultant to set up an initial meeting. After the first meeting, the contact with regard to the meeting's time would be between the consultant and the player. We decided on a monthly meeting with the director and social worker for updates and brainstorming on various issues. In addition, once a month the sport psychology consultants took part in a joint meeting with the academy administration and the medical staff from the Ribstein Center. The aim of these meetings was to report on and hear about the physiological, psychological, nutritional, medical, and pedagogical state of the players. The academy basketball team is financially supported by the Basketball Federation and the Wingate Institute administration.

Sport psychology consultants – Coaching staff: In an academy setting, players often approach the coach when they encounter a problem or some kind of obstacle. Therefore, the coach should be empathic and reassuring, using positive rather than negative communication, and have good listening skills. Beyond the traditional role of the coach, in the academy setting the coach serves as an educator, and must be aware of the psychosocial and physical aspects of the players' growth and development. In line with this perspective, sport psychology consultants need to cooperate with the coaching staff. For example, the coach consults with the sport psychologist about individual and team problems, they make decisions together, and discuss various possibilities of applying their decisions in an effective way. Another example of this cooperation is how the sport psychology consultant explains the psychological context of the problem to the coach, as well as ways to resolve the conflict. BB and IO provided the coach with suggestions on how to achieve effective communication with the players, assistant coach, staff, and parents, and ideas about various ways to resolve ongoing issues. A real-life example is when the coach approached the sport psychologist and shared with him a comment he heard from one of the key players. The team captain told the coach: "I am not having fun. Please help me". The coach recommended that the player to talk with the consultant. The player followed the coach's advice and started individual meetings with the sport psychology consultant. We analyzed the situation with the captain and the coach, observed some games and training sessions to collect some information, and developed programs to improve team dynamics and cohesion. This model of interaction and open relationship with the coach-player-sport psychologist was very effective, also in future cooperation. The core of the relationship with the basketball team was the interaction between the consultant and the coach – it included various types of communication, such as individual meetings, phone calls, e-mails, SMS's, etc. In this case, both sides – the consultant and the coach – were satisfied with the interaction and the impact of the relationship on their professional development.

Sport psychology consultants – Players: The interaction with the team was provided via three main models: Long-term psychological skills training with some players, short-term psychological support according to player's or coach's request; and situational psychological support.

Long term psychological training sessions included individual meetings with seven players. We provided team training sessions in which the focus was on cohesion and team dynamics. A basic skill which we taught the players was improving their decision-making process, not only during the game but also in life perspective issues, such as whether or not to stay in the academy. This skill was essential, since some players received invitations from outside clubs that offered better conditions. Beyond that, we met with the players and worked on individual programs in which they learned psychological skills based on their specific needs. Some of the mental skills they learned were concentration, self-regulation, self-confidence, imagery, and a regulation exercise with GSR/EMG BFB. A typical individual session was composed of three parts: introduction, basic work, and final part. In the *introduction* (short talk of 3-5 min.) we focused on current national, individual, and team news. In *basic work* psychological skill training was provided with BFB devices and VCR, focusing on concentration, imagery, attention focusing, and relaxation-excitation waves (Blumenstein and Bar-Eli, 2005; Blumenstein and Weinstein, 2010). In the *final* part, relaxation with music was provided (short muscle relaxation for 3-5 min). Some of the players were instructed to also use a self-talk and pre-competitive routine in order to help them create or adapt to new tactical plays. The team mental training sessions were provided in order to develop a positive team approach and to facilitate team building. Team sessions were conducted before or after practice in a training hall. We discussed with the players topics such as communication in games, team concentration, sportsmanship, and leadership in team. Every team session ended with 10 minutes of relaxation.

During team sessions one important topic was frequently raised: What is more important? The team's "way" or team results (win-lose)? Is winning everything? After thorough discussions we established a core norm which focused on the "way", which means emphasizing developing skills and giving maximum effort during practices and games. It was agreed that if the player gives all his efforts he will never be a loser. If the team loses it only reflects the team's current state, and this should motivate players to work harder.

During our team meetings a main goal was to improve team cohesion. This was done by focusing on three ways to achieve it. The first was recognizing the uniqueness of the basketball team, which in our case was the first academy team in basketball. The second was developing individual and team norms (e.g., educational, training, behavior). The third was emphasizing interaction and communication between the players inside and outside basketball, in order to develop "brotherhood" among the players.

Short-term psychological support according to the players' or coachs' request. One of the players had sleeping problems and approached the social worker, who recommended that he meet with BB. The sport psychology consultant analyzed the daily routine of the player. Practice finished around 20:30, then he went to the dining room, and only then around 22:00 did he go to sleep. The routine did not help the player to relax; therefore the consultant taught him relaxation skills and modified the schedule after evening practice. After dinner, it was recommended that he take a short 20-30 min walk, while focusing on the way he felt during the walk and not on outside issues. In the end, the player was able to fall asleep while doing relaxation and focusing on positive thinking that was related to his day. Finally, the player normalized his sleeping process.

Another example reflected the coach's plan to provide one of his centers with more playing time and to demands more cooperation with another player-center. Therefore, as a consequence, the sport psychologist consultant was asked to spend more time with the players, mentally preparing them for this change. Moreover, the sport psychology consultant was asked to conduct some sessions in which the two centers would participate together to improve their communication and to discuss different game situations.

Situational psychological support. This is illustrated by the following scenario: During one of the games the coach was upset with a player and took him out of the game before the third quarter. The player reacted with strong emotions (anger, sadness). BB spoke with the player, and reminded him how to relax and concentrate more on performance and less on emotions. After a few minutes the player started to warm up and observe the game. BB directed the player to focus on coach's instructions, and finally he was ready to go back into the game. The coach was aware of the player's readiness, and after some time asked the player to return to the game. The player had a great comeback on the court. After the game, the player thanked BB and apologized to the coach. Another example of situational psychological support occurred when the coach was upset with his players' performance during an official game and lost his temper. The players reacted with strong emotions, and as a consequence were afraid to make mistakes. Therefore, the players could not perform well. BB approached the coach and told him (only to the coach's ears) that if he did not relaxed and change his behavior his players might lose the game, since they were not receiving clear recommendations from him. The players couldn't understand the coach's reactions. The coach calmed down and corrected his behavior. As a consequence the players felt the change that occurred in the coach, and were able to come back and win the game! After the game, the coach thanked BB for his help.

Sport psychologist consultants – Parents. The climate in which we worked with the basketball team in the academy was characterized by the parents' two major expectations: the educational process and sport results for their child's future career. Therefore, there was a great deal of pressure from the parents' side regarding players' achievements in school and in sport. For some parents the future sport career was very important, and this was revealed by game attendance, interaction with the consultant by phone, involvement with the coach, and keeping updated regarding their child's progress. On the other hand, some parents viewed the academy experience as a tool for developing their child's skills for future achievements, not necessarily in sport. An important component of our philosophy was to enable stable and strong cooperation between the coach (academy) and the parents. To accomplish this we guided the coach on listening and evaluation skills to be used when interacting with parents. This means that the coach listened to the parent's request but he evaluated each one using his professional skills and experience, whether or not the parent's request was legitimate. The message the parents received was that they were being listened to, but also that they had to respect the coach's approach and final decision. In line with this, several individual and team meetings with the parents in attendance were provided. For example, when the sport psychology consultant realized that most parents would be attending the U16 Men's European Championship Men, Montenegro 2010, we invited the parents for two meetings. The meetings had two major goals. One goal was to talk about the expectations the coach had from the parents regarding their involvement during the two-week tournament. Some of the guidelines were that the parents would stay in a different hotel and that they were limited in the visit and interaction times they were allowed with the players. Other guidelines were about expected behavior before, during, and after games, specific free days to spend with the players, etc.

The second goal was to discuss, explain, and guide the parents on how to support the player at home while he was trying to coping with competitive stress. The consultants presented the parents with issues such as pre-competitive routine, concentration, and motivation. After the meeting there were many individual questions from the parents regarding personal concerns related to their kids and their family situation. More details on this topic will be discussed in the next chapter: PST for Youth Sport.

CONCLUSION

To summarize this chapter, there are major conclusions to be made.

First, it is necessary to have full cooperation between the psychological skill consultants and the coaching staff.

Second, in professional team sport the emphasis is on mental practice skills, oriented for sport results. However, in youth team sport, in addition to the sport process and the results, mental practice skills are also orientated toward educational achievements.

Third, a good start for beginning cooperation with a professional team is the training camp model. For youth teams, one recommendation is building the relationship over a longer period that may last for several months.

Fourth, the psychological skill training with the team is provided in both an individual and team manner.

REFERENCES

Blumenstein, B., and Bar-Eli, M. (2005). Biofeedback applications in sport. In D. Hackfort, J. Duda, and R. Lidor (Eds.). *Handbook of research in applied sport and exercise psychology: International perspectives* (pp. 185-198). Morgantown, WV. Fitness Information Technology.

Blumenstein, B., Bar-Eli, M., and Collins, D. (2002). Biofeedback training in sport. In B. Blumenstein, M. Bar-Eli, and G. Tenenbaum (Eds.). *Brain and body in sport and exercise: Biofeedback applications in performance enhancement* (pp. 55-76). Chichester, UK: Wiley.

Blumenstein, B., and Weinstein, Y. (2010). *Psychological skills training: Application to elite sport performance*. Grand Rapids, MI: Ultimate Athlete Concepts.

Burke, K. L. (2006). Using sport psychology to improve basketball performance. In J. Dosil (Ed.), *The sport psychologist's handbook: A guide for sport-specific performance enhancement* (pp. 121-138). Chichester, West Sussex: Wiley.

Dosil, J. (Ed.) (2006). Psychological intervention with football (soccer) teams. In J. Dosil (Ed.), *The sport psychologist's handbook: A guide for sport-specific performance enhancement* (pp. 139-158). Chichester, West Sussex: Wiley.

Hall, C. R. (2001). Imagery in sport and exercise. In R. N. Singer, H. A. Hausenblas, and C.M. Janelle (Eds.), *Handbook of sport psychology* (2nd ed., pp. 529-549). New York: Wiley.

Henschen, K. (2005). Mental practice-skill oriented. In D. Hackfort, J. Duda, and R. Lidor (Eds.). *Handbook of research in applied sport and exercise psychology: International perspectives* (pp. 19-36). Morgantown, WV: Fitness Information Technology.

Henschen, K .P., and Cook, D. (2003). Working with professional basketball players. In R. Lidor and K. P. Henschen (Eds.), *The psychology of team sports* (pp. 143-160). Morgantown, WV: Fitness Information Technology.

Lidor, R., Blumenstein, B., and Tenenbaum, G. (2007). Psychological aspects of training programs in European basketball: Conceptualization, periodization, and planning. *The Sport Psychologist, 21*(3), 353-367.

Moran, A. P. (2003). Improving concentration skills in team-sport performers: Focusing techniques for soccer players. In R. Lidor and K. P. Henschen (Eds.), *The psychology of team sports* (pp. 161-189). Morgantown, WV: Fitness Information Technology.

Moran, A. (2005). Training attention and concentration skills in athletes. In D. Hackfort, J. Duda, and R. Lidor (Eds.). *Handbook of research in applied sport and exercise psychology: International perspectives* (pp. 61-74). Morgantown, WV: Fitness Information Technology.

Tuckman, B. W. (1965). Development sequence in small groups. *Psychological Bulletin*, 63, 384-399.

Tuckman, B. W., and Jensen, M. A. C. (1977). Stages of small group development revisited. *Group and Organizational Studies, 2,* 419-427.

Wooden, J. R. (1980). *Practical modern basketball* (2nd ed.). New York: Wiley.

Chapter 5

PSYCHOLOGICAL SKILLS TRAINING WITH YOUTH ATHLETES

ABSTRACT

This chapter will propose our educational approach with youth athletes (age 13-18 years) from sport academy and sport federations, in which the coaching staff, parents, administration, and sport psychology consultants (SPC) are part of the team working together to achieve common goals. The authors focused on psychological skills training (PST) for individual (tennis, table tennis, judo) and team sports (basketball). The uniqueness of the following PST programs for youth athletes were the duration (short and long-term), gender (male and female), and SPC-parent relationship. Due to the young age of the athletes a special emphasis is given to the relationship between the coach and the parents.

INTRODUCTION

We perceive the young athlete as a future professional athlete who needs extensive scientific and medical support while taking into account specific parameters, such as age, physiological and psychological maturation, environment, and personal development. When working with youth athletes in the *sport academy* there are a few considerations that should be taken into account. First, PST for youth athletes, especially in the beginning, should focus on personal development rather than performance enhancement. The challenge for the athlete is to maintain high sport motivation and minimize the importance of the outcome, while giving maximum effort in each training exercise. Second, the psychological consultants should take into account the effect and the interaction parents have on the players and coaching staff. Third, mental strategies such as biofeedback (BFB) training, self-talk, goal setting, mental imagery, relaxation, and attention control should be modified according to the capabilities of the young athletes (Chase, 2010; Smoll, 2001; Tremayne and Newbery, 2005; Weiss, 1991). Fourth, while working with young athletes there is an additional advantage to PST – the skills the young athletes acquire will benefit him throughout his/her sport career. It is recommended that the athlete become familiar with PST at a young age rather than later in his/her career.

When working with youth athletes from *sport federations* or *clubs*, there are some variables that the SPC should consider. First, the reason that the young athlete has started the consulting might be coach's recommendation, the parents' initiative to support their kids, or a need for mental support before an important competition. Second, usually the consulting lasts for only a short term period. After experiencing positive performance results, the athlete and parents may discontinue cooperation with the SPC. Why? (1) The cost of consulting might be difficult for the parents to pay for a long period without any external support; (2) Perhaps it is difficult for the athlete to come to meetings each week while adhering to the training schedule; (3) The belief that after experiencing positive performance results the athlete can regulate and cope with competitive demands successfully on his/her own. Third, regular contact each week will be with the parents, therefore it is important to be aware of the type of parents with whom you are communicating. According to Smoll (2001) parents can be classified as follows:

1. Disinterested parents are those who are not involved with their kids' sports activities.
2. Overcritical parents are those who are never satisfied with their kids' achievements.
3. Screaming parents are those who interfering through their "vocal" comments.
4. Overprotective parents are those who are excessively worried about their kids.
5. Sideline coaches are those parents who assume the coach's role.

What coach and sport psychological consultant should do will be reflected in the following cases.

CASE 13: TENNIS – LONG-TERM COOPERATION WITH AN ATHLETE AND HIS FATHER

In November 2007, a young tennis player, age 13, entered the sport academy. His father came to BB's office and asked BB to work with his child for psychological support. The father told BB that his child was afraid to lose and therefore his game was very cautious. In addition, the child was not mentally tough and was being influenced by opponents, and due to these reason he did not put all effort into what was needed, and gave up when facing obstacles. Overall, the child was not emotionally stable during training and competitions. The father characterized the child as an athlete with high talent and potential but without confidence in his future. The father promised to stay in touch with BB and keep him updated regarding the player. According to Smoll (2001) this father can be classified as a combination of an "overprotective parent" and a "sideline coach".

BB met with the child and discovered that he had high motivation, wanted to achieve professional status in tennis, was ready for hard training, and was willing to work with the Olympic SPC. Next, BB met with the coach so that they could determine together realistic goals for the child. BB agreed with the coach that he would visit the practice once a week and have weekly meetings with the player.

The first goal BB gave the player was to train during the first month with maximum effort and intensity in each exercise, and not to let subjective and external factors such as mood and climate interfere with his training. During that month BB visited the practice once a week, interacted with the athlete and the coach, and observed the player's behavior. In addition, the father kept in close touch with the consultant, but was impatient regarding BB's approach. In order to calm the father BB provided him with some details regarding his mental plan and work with the athlete. Moreover, BB asked the father not to get involved during competitions and training. At the end of the month the athlete reported on achieving the goal of training hard, and therefore the next step of the psychological support would begin – the learning and developing of psychological strategies and skills. This stage lasted throughout the year 2008. The psychological strategies BB and the athlete worked on were the W5SA (Blumenstein, Bar-Eli, and Collins, 2002; Blumenstein, Bar-Eli, and Tenenbaum, 1997), self-talk (Henschen, 2005; Zinsser, Bunker, and Williams, 2001), goal setting (Gould, 2006), relaxation (Henschen, 2005; Williams and Harris, 2001), concentration and attention control (Moran, 2005; Nideffer and

Table 5.1. Player's Self-estimation of his Effort (E), Motivation (M1), and Mood (M2) during Practice in the Year 2008

	Jan	Feb.	Mar	Apr	May	June	July	Aug	Sept	Oct.	Nov	Dec
E	4.0	3.7	4.0	4.5	4.5	4.7	4.5	5.0	4.7	5.0	4.7	4.5
M1	3.7	4.0	4.2	4.0	4.2	4.5	4.2	4.7	4.0	4.5	4.5	4.7
M2	3.2	3.5	4.2	4.2	3.7	4.2	3.5	4.5	4.2	3.2	4.5	4.5

Sagal, 2001). In addition, a special relationship was built up between the athlete and the consultant. Beyond mental skills the consultant discussed with the athlete topics such as ethical norms in sport and tennis, the importance of education and behavior outside the court, and direct assistance in school such as math and English (especially after trips abroad). In addition, to keep the athlete focused on his effort and mental state, he was asked by the consultant to evaluate himself after each practice on his level of motivation, effort, and mood on a Likert-type scale (1– low to 5–high). The requirement was that effort would be always high (4-5). Every week the athlete gave BB a report on his achievements (see Table 5.1). It is interesting to note that although mood was sometime in the middle (3), effort and motivation were still high (4-5). This led BB to conclude that the athlete was mentally tough and that he understood the importance of high effort for future performance. During the first year the father called BB about two times each week to get updated regarding his son's progress and his achievements in tennis matches. After conversations with BB, during which the father began to understand his negative impact on his child's performance, he decreased the frequency of his communications with BB to once a month and significantly changed his behavior during training and competitions. The player finished the year in tenth place in the Israeli classification.

In the year 2009, when the tennis player was 14 years old, BB continued the psychological meetings with him once a week, and focused on applying psychological techniques in training and competitions, especially developing a pre-competitive routine, relaxation between games, and concentration before each point. BB continued to keep up his good relations with the coach, attending practice sessions once per week, and he met with the player's father once per month. An important point for that year was the mental toughness the athlete exhibited. He won matches against players who had beaten him in the past, he was able to come back during matches in which he was behind, and he took critical points in the games. When analyzing the matches, the player emphasized the importance of the concentration and relaxation skills he had

**Table 5.2. Description of Psychological Work
with the Tennis Player throughout 2008-2010**

	20008 (mainly in laboratory setting)	2009 (laboratory and training setting)	2010 (situational training)
Goals	Maximum effort and intensity in each exercise Stable avoidance from external interference	Develop psychological skills with stress factors	Stability in games Applying psychological skills in competition
Psychological Intervention	W5SA Self-talk Goal setting Muscle relaxation Concentration	Pre-competitive routine Applying psychological techniques in training (self-talk, goal setting, muscle relaxation, concentration)	Applying psychological techniques in different situations: Between sets, win/lose, before serve, after mistake, etc.
Achievements	Tenth, Israeli classification	Fifth, Israeli classification 30th, European classification	First, Israeli classification Tenth, European classification

learned during his work with the consultant. In this year the player achieved fifth place in the Israeli classification and 30th in the European classification. One obstacle faced was inconsistency in the schedule of consultation meetings, since the player was often abroad for training camps and competitions. Therefore, when the player was in Israel the meetings were held twice a week.

The year 2010, when the player was 15 years old, started with high expectations, optimism, and motivation. The main focus of the SPC's work was on competitive behavior and mental strategies in a variety of stressful situations, such as the following:

The beginning of the match: The player should give special attention to the mental parameters of self-confidence, muscle relaxation, and concentration.

In-between sets: The player's behavior is dependent on the situation he is facing. In the case of being behind (losing), the player should use muscle relaxation, self-talk, and concentration skills.

During the mental consultation meetings the player trained in these skills while being exposed to audio and visual simulation of stressful conditions (Blumenstein and Weinstein, 2010). When the player was in *advantage (winning)*, he should use psychological skills such as arousal regulations, self-talk, and concentration skills, with the goal of keeping himself at the optimal state. The player's achievements were being the first in his age group in the Israeli classification and tenth in the European classification (fourth in the European classification in April of 2011). Moreover, he received 55 points in the World classification of up to age 18. The player's father did not call BB during the last year, since he had confidence in his son's progress and achievements. Table 5.2 presents the goals, psychological strategies, and achievements of the player over three years.

Today BB meets with the player only occasionally, because the player is abroad most of the time, but when he practices at the Wingate Institute he always come to BB's office to discuss his latest news or to receive a necessary consultation.

CASE 14: TABLE TENNIS – ONE-YEAR COOPERATION WITH A 14 YEAR-OLD GIRL

This story took place during the year of 2008/9 at the Wingate Institute, at the sport academy. The girl was one of the best table tennis players in Israel, and lived in a small town in a remote location in the north of Israel. She joined the academy with the goal of acquiring professional skills and experience. However, the adjustment was not easy for her, since from being the star of the town she had to "fight" for her status in the academy with many other talented players. Beyond that the player had to deal with new surroundings and certain demands she was not used to, which had an effect on her relationship with the coach and the other players, and her overall behavior. She exhibited aggressive behavior towards her coach, her teachers, and her friends. As a consequence, the player started to consider the option of withdrawing from the academy and going back home. The academy director approached BB and asked him to meet with the player. After two sessions BB felt that the player would better benefit from a female consultant, and recommended that she meet with IO. This was the beginning of a long-term relationship that lasted throughout the year. IO met with the player and spoke with her mother. The initial purpose was to get to know the player on different levels, such as sport, education, social, etc. This was achieved by discussions with the coach, teacher, and her mom. They all described the player as a motivated and talented player who was very easily affected by emotions, and who reacted with aggressive speech and behavior, impatience, and relatively low self-confidence. At the first meeting IO and the player understood each other and felt they could work together. There was good chemistry between them, and the overall feeling was of optimism, readiness to cooperate, and openness. The first issue was the decision making regarding continuation at the academy. Therefore, during the first stage IO worked with the player on the process of decision making. The player was emotional, and that had an effect on her performance in school and at training, and on her relationship with friends and the coaching staff. In the first nine meetings the emphasis was on teaching the player techniques of relaxation, self-regulation, and BFB training. Regarding her conflict of whether or not to stay at the academy, she decided not to make a decision until December. This decision had a positive effect and reduced the tension she was experiencing, since "not to make a decision" was also a decision. When the emotional state of the player stabilized, the consultant started to talk again with her about continuing the process of decision making. The method was based on the cognitive approach of goal setting. The player's main goal was playing on the Israeli National team by the end of the season. Then, IO analyzed the road map to achieve this goal, going from the farthest point in time until the present (Figure 5.1).

The player realized that in order to achieve the main goal she had to stay in the academy. Once she recognized the importance of playing in the academy, her decision making during the ninth meeting was easier and "emotion"-free. Ultimately, the player decided to stay at the academy.

Figure 5.1. The road map of decision making for the tennis player.

The main emphasis of the second stage, which lasted for 10 meetings, was on preparing the athlete for several competitions. The consultant work during these meeting was focused on self-regulation skills, behavioral modification (anger control, high confidence), developing a pre-competitive routine, and communication with the coaching staff and referee before and during competitions.

During the meetings IO realized that the player's cognitive evaluation of her outcomes was not effective, meaning that the reasons she chose for her outcomes had a negative influence on her motivation The player was influenced by external parameters such as competitors' behavior, referee decisions, coach's comments, etc. Her self-confidence and motivation were greatly influenced by those factors. Therefore, for the next few meetings IO taught the player how to evaluate her outcomes based on the principles of attribution training (Biddle, 1993; Weiner, 1986). The main issue was choosing reasons that are internal and are under the control of the player. For example, when the player had a bad match, she had the tendency to attribute her performance to reasons such as "I am not good enough" or "As usual, I lost my temper and I reacted". Those sentences made the player believe that she could not change the reasons for her behavior, and therefore her motivation and self-confidence were low. However, during the meetings with IO they evaluated the situations, and IO led the player to realize that there might be other reasons for the outcomes that can be controlled and changed by her. For example, the player focused on her ability to control her temper and improve her playing quality by learning how to self-regulate herself, prepare a routine, focusing reactions to situations in which she was losing her concentration, etc. This cognitive mode had a positive effect on the player's motivation and self-confidence, since she learned tools she could use when she felt it to be necessary. She felt in control of her playing quality (Figure 5.2).

In addition to evaluating bad performance, IO and the player worked on evaluating good performance (Figure 5.3). The focus was on attributing success to internal reasons, in order to increase feelings of pride. As can be seen in Figure 5.2, when analyzing performance it is important to emphasize reasons that are under the control of the player, in order to increase high motivation and the feeling of control. The player learned to use attributes such as being prepared, raising her concentration level, and maintaining overall readiness for her performance. The player believed that she could change and control those reasons; therefore, even after a bad performance she kept up her positive attitude and high motivation. The player practiced the above cognitive evaluation during practice and later on after competition.

Figure 5.2. Effective and ineffective cognitive process after bad performance in table tennis.

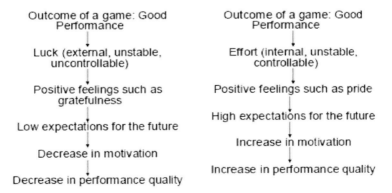

Figure 5.3. Effective and ineffective cognitive process after good performance in table tennis.

As can be seen in Figure 5.3, the player learned that even after success it is important to pay attention to the reasons she used to explain her performance. In order to increase feelings of pride and high motivation, the player learned to use internal attributes such as ability, effort, self-regulation, concentration, etc.

Overall, the attribution training in the cognitive process is an important skill for teaching young athletes, since it has an overall effect on mental parameters such as feelings, expectations, adherence, and motivation. This kind of thinking process is the basis on which other mental parameters can be developed in the future.

After several months the player competed in an important competition, in which she achieved second place. This was a positive result after a long, unsuccessful period. This outcome significantly influenced the athlete's behavior, mood, and motivation. In the following competition (Israeli championship) the player achieved first place, and due to this she was selected to the national team. In the next month the player was invited to a few European training camps and competitions abroad. The overall feeling and mood was extremely positive.

Moreover, there was a significant improvement in the players' behavior and attitude. Her coping skills during school, practice, and competitions were greatly improved. She felt confident in her decision making skills and continued to live and train at the sport academy. However, after a year, due to family reasons, the player went back home and trained irregularly with the local club. Since then she has not achieved any significant results.

CASE 15: BASKETBALL – ONE-YEAR COOPERATION FOR BEHAVIOR MODIFICATION

This case study is about a 14 year-old boy and his mother, who called BB and asked for his professional consultation. The boy was an excellent basketball player, playing in the youth league. The mother had high aspirations for her son to achieve the status of professional basketball player in the future. The main reason for approaching BB was due to the boy's behavior in school. He was aggressive in school, had a negative relationship with the teacher and the other kids, and got low grades. The goal was to help the boy change his behavior in order to improve conduct and relationships, especially in school. After the first meeting, BB presented the following program to the boy. The main point was that BB would help the boy to develop his psychological skills for improving basketball performance, and that the boy would improve his behavior in school by practicing these skills there as well. Their mutual work lasted from October 2009 until September 2010, once per week, 55 minutes per meeting. In addition, BB was in a regular contact with the mother through phone calls. In the first two months (October-November) BB taught the boy fundamental psychological techniques, such as muscle relaxation, concentration, and BFB training using the short-version of the W5SA. The boy enjoyed the meetings and was proud of his achievements.

After mastering the fundamental psychological skills, the boy attempted to gradually use these skills in the classroom. The school served as a training ground for testing the boy's level of understanding and ability of the psychological skills. One of the conditions between BB and the boy was that by using self-regulation skills the boy had to stay "quiet" and answer only the teacher's questions. BB asked the mother to call any time there was any conflict or a problem with the boy. Before the meetings started, the boy had incidents in school on a daily basis; most of the time he was the initiator of the conflicts. However, after two months of cooperation the mother called BB only twice (in November) to report on incidents in which the boy was not even the initiator. According to the mother and the teacher, the boy improved his behavior significantly. For example, during the following seven months the boy was involved in only three minor incidents.

During our work we focused on the player's basketball performance, in addition to developing his psychological skills. In December-January BB and the boy worked intensively on concentration and self-regulation with stress distraction, such as positive/negative verbal motivation and applied concentration and self-regulation under competitive noises. In February-March imagery skills were practiced, especially defense and attack combinations in the laboratory setting. In this period BB visited the boy's games and connected with his coach. To BB's surprise, the boy did not have any problems with the coach or the other players. The opposite – he was a play-maker. In April-May the boy played four important games with his team in which he improved his scoring and achieved 12-14 points per game, versus 6-7 points before his cooperation with BB began. In addition, the boy demonstrated leadership abilities.

In the summer the boy participated in an international basketball training camp for two months, and the connection with BB was only through phone calls. In September, BB met with the mother and the boy to discuss his current state and future goals. Due to financial limitations the mother could not continue with regular meetings. After a few months with no consultation and support the boy started to take medication to control his behavior and concentration.

Psychological skill training helped the athlete to improve his basketball performance and had a positive effect on his behavior in school. However, like physical training, when you stop practice your skills deteriorate. The boy had to continue his psychological support in order to maintain his behavior level.

Most of the previous case studies presented in this book have been based on long-term cooperation with a SPC. However, there are cases in youth sport in which the consultation is provided for a short time period, or is non–systematic, as can be seen in the following two case studies.

CASE 16: BASKETBALL – SHORT-TERM COOPERATION (TWO MONTHS) FOR PERFORMANCE ENHANCEMENT

This short story is about a 16 year-old basketball player who played in the youth league and had practiced for the last eight years. The boy's mother called BB, described the reasons for initiating the consultation, and requested psychological support for her son. The boy was an only child, used to being the center of the family, and was sensitive to external influences in sport such as crowd behavior, the coach's comments during and after the game, and overall behavior. When the player over-analyzed a situation his play was at its lowest level. In a good game the boy scored 6-7 points in a game. The goal for the consultation meetings was to prepare for an upcoming significant game the next month.

In the *first meeting*, we tested the player's mental qualities in the lab and diagnosed the boy as a person with low self-confidence, but with fast and good concentration and muscle relaxation in a sterile situation (silence). However, when external and outside stimuli were presented, the boy's concentration and muscle relaxation deteriorated. He got "stressed–out" and his decision making abilities were ineffective. BB's goal was to strengthen the boy's concentration skills and to adapt them to external distractors such as coach's remarks, fans' reactions, and competition noises.

During the *second meeting* BB worked on teaching the player concentration and relaxation skills using Electromyography and Galvanic Skin Response (EMG/ GSR) BFB, controlled for different situations. One situation was based on external signals given by BB in which the player must immediately concentrate. The player could observe the success of his GSR reaction on the computer screen .Another situation on which the player practiced was short and fast concentration, in which the player was requested to fully concentrate for 5-10 seconds. Last situation was negative and positive comments given to the player by BB during short concentration drills. For example, negative comments can be "it is not your day, you are performing badly, and you don't have it", and positive comments can be "great, you can do it, excellent performance". In this meeting the player strengthened his concentration skills and self-confidence levels. The player could observe all his behavior on the computer screen and therefore he believed in the process, which is based on objective measures.

The *third meeting* started with the same concentration exercise, and after a short warm-up a few demands were added. For example, the player had to achieve a specific level of concentration during 5-10-20 seconds. In addition, imagery was provided as well. The imagery was oriented through the technical and tactical sides of performance. For example, he played in defense (zone or personal) and attack. The player was asked to image a variety of situations in which he played, including making 20 attempts from the foul line.

The player's pre-competitive routine was developed in the *fourth meeting*, including situations such as the beginning of the game, the waiting period while sitting on the bench, the period before the game and the warm-up. BB worked on the player's self-talking and positive thinking. Lastly, imagery was provided with real competitive noise and TV films.

During the *fifth* and the *sixth meetings* the same model that was initially used in the fourth meeting was strengthened. However, the imagery was harder since the player was asked to image while playing against a concrete team that he was scheduled to play against.

In the *seventh meeting* the athlete practiced on his foul-line throws in stressful situations, such as when the score is very close and the player is going to the foul line a few seconds before the game is over. Another situation in which the stress is greater is when your team is losing by one point and you are going to the foul line a few seconds before the game is over.

The boy felt ready for the upcoming game. After the game the mother called and reported that the boy had an excellent performance: A total of 16 points, with six points from the foul line. The mother thanked BB and terminated the consultation.

CASE 17: JUDO – NON-SYSTEMATIC COOPERATION WITH A YOUNG JUDOKA

The story began with a meeting in BB's office with the judoka (18 year-old, female) and her coach. The judoka had a negative perspective and spoke in a disparaging way in regard to her performance, practice exercise, and future achievements. In addition, communication between the judoka and her coach was not stable or productive. Moreover, the judoka had a negative perspective on psychological knowledge, since, as she said, "Psychology is a science without measurements, it is only talking". On the other hand, the judoka had a good judo basis, performed her exercises precisely and with a great deal of power and speed. The judoka was not sure about to her weight level, which caused a lot of tension. BB connected with a sport nutritionist who recommended that the judoka focus on a weight level of 52 kg. Once the judoka accepted her weight category, it helped her to plan her practice and to anticipate her main present and future competitors . The impact of this on her training was significant, since the judoka was more concentrated, relaxed, and in control. This step already helped in building the rapport between BB and the judoka, since she realized that BB was not just a man of words but also a man of action.

During the initial meetings BB introduced the judoka to the BFB device (HR, EMG, and GSR) and to different BFB games. The precise numbers gave the judoka objective information about her concentration and self-regulation skills. For example, the results of the judoka's first SRT from the W5SA (see Chapter 1) are presented in Table 5.3.

Based on the results (only 7+ from 12+ maximum), BB concluded that this athlete had a low self-regulation level, and especially that the reactions of EMG and GSR needed to be improved. Similar results were with RTP: In exercise 10 (simple) – 20 (Choice) – 20 (Discrimination): 214 – 216 - 204 msc. The first effect from these measurements was very significant for this

Table 5.3. The First Self-regulation Test Results of the Judoka

	Rest	Tension	Relaxation	Competition
HR bpm	56-66 +	62-64	60-54 +	62-76 +
EMG µV	2.2-2.0	2.1-2.4	2.6-2.0 +	2.4-3.2 +
GSR kΩ	235-220	218-310 +	280-260	255-150 +

judoka, since it was possible for her to quantify her performance during the psychological consultation. She was interested in knowing her performance in regard to other judokas, and wanted to set performance goals that would prepare her to be mentally ready for competition. The data were a motivator for the judoka to continue psychological skill training. We used our traditional psychological skill program for combat sport (see Chapter 2 for more details).

An important aspect of the training was the involvement of the coach during the meetings with BB (April-May). BB asked the coach to join them while the judoka practiced her mental readiness using imagery. The coach gave comments to the judoka during the imagery, strengthening the vividness of the imagery scene by giving technical-tactical comments against concrete opponents, similar to a real-life match. As a by-product this experience improved the relationship between the coach and the judoka, along with increasing the professionalism of the coach.

In August 2008, before the World Junior Judo Championship (in Thailand), the judoka achieved 15-30-30: simple-169 (ratio: 9 fast/6 slow), choice-185 (ratio: 10 fast/5 slow), descrimination-175 (ratio: 9 fast/6 slow) in RTP. In the event, the judoka achieved her first silver medal in a World Championship. In January 2009 the Judoka traveled with the junior judo team to a training camp for one month in Japan. The psychological consultation resumed from March 2009, 3-4 times per month, with periodic pauses due to international competitions. During meetings BB applied the traditional program for combat sports, but with a focus on using different stress factors such as competitive noises, film fragments, physical contact, and specific demands. An example of a modified technique that was sport–specific is the relaxation exercise the judoka performed for 1, 3, and 5 min with external stress and fast concentration for 10, 20, and 30 sec. Similar to the previous year, the judoka practiced an imagery scene for 5 min, the same length as the actual match. During the imagery the coach made specific comments to the judoka. BB added another demand by asking the judoka to give a finger signal every time she made an attack. The number of attacks per minute were recorded, and then analyzed together with the coach. In addition, during the meetings BB focused on improving a pre-competitive routine, which included fast relaxation, fast concentration, positive thinking, performance goals, self-regulation, and effective decision-making. In August 2009, before the World Junior Judo Championship in Paris, the judoka asked BB to conduct an RTP test to evaluate her progress compared to the results from the previous year. The progress of the RTS's results starting from the first meeting are presented in Table 5.4.

**Table 5.4. The Judoka's RTP's Results
throughout the Psychological Consultation**

	Simple	Choice	Discrimination
First Meeting	214 ms (ratio: fast 4/slow 11)	216 ms (ratio: fast 2/slow 13)	204 ms (ratio: fast 3/slow 12)
After Two Months	183 ms (ratio: fast 5/slow 10)	196 ms (ratio: fast 6/slow 9)	194 ms (ratio: fast 6/slow 9)
Before WC* in Thailand, August 2008	169 ms (ratio: fast 9/slow 6)	185 ms (ratio: fast 10/slow 5)	175 ms (ratio: fast 9/slow 6)
Before WC in Paris, August 2009	165 ms (ratio: fast 10/slow 5)	175 ms (ratio: fast 9/slow 6)	170 ms (ratio: fast 10/slow 5)

WC* = World Championship

In Paris in 2009 the judoka won the silver medal. The cooperation between the judoka and BB continues to the present, with the goal of achieving a place in the Israeli delegation to the Olympic Games in London 2012.

CONCLUSION

To summarize this chapter:

- Psychological support is an important tool for keeping youth athletes in sport and for ensuring solid and healthy continuation.
- The psychological consultation has an effect on behavior outside of sport.
- Many times, the initial contact is made by the parents, usually the mother, and often the initial positive results can fulfill the goal of the client.
- SPCs should encourage cooperation and contact with the parents, even more than with the coach.
- It is important to start psychological consultation in a young age, since there are cases in which the consultation can determine the quality and future of the athlete's career.

REFERENCES

Biddle, S. (1993) Attribution research and sport psychology. In R. Singer, M. Murphy, and L. Tennant (Eds.) *Handbook of research in sport psychology* (pp.437-464). NY: Macmillan.

Blumenstein, B., Bar-Eli, M., and Collins, D. (2002). Biofeedback training in sport. In B. Blumenstein, M. Bar-Eli, and G. Tenenbaum (Eds.). *Brain and body in sport and exercise: Biofeedback applications in performance enhancement* (pp. 55-76). Chichester, UK: Wiley.

Blumenstein, B., Bar-Eli, M., and Tenenbaum, G. (1997). A five step approach to mental training incorporating biofeedback. *The Sport Psychologist, 11*, 440-453.

Blumenstein, B. and Weinstein, Y. (2010). *Psychological skills training: Application to elite sport performance.* Grand Rapids, MI: Ultimate Athlete Concepts.

Chase, M. (2010). Children. In S. Hanrahan and M. Andersen (Eds.), *Routledge handbook of applied sport psychology: A comprehensive guide for students and practitioners* (pp. 377-386). London and New York: Routledge, Taylor and Francis Group.

Gould, D. (2006). Goal setting for peak performance. In J. Williams (Ed.), *Applied sport psychology: Personal growth to peak performance* (5th ed., pp. 240-259). Boston: McGraw-Hill.

Henschen, K. (2005). Mental practice-skill oriented. In D. Hackfort, J. Duda, and R. Lidor (Eds.). *Handbook of research in applied sport and exercise psychology: International perspectives* (pp. 19-36). Morgantown, WV: Fitness Information Technology.

Moran, A. (2005). Training attention and concentration skills in athletes. In D. Hackfort, J. Duda, and R. Lidor (Eds.). *Handbook of research in applied sport and exercise psychology: International perspectives* (pp. 61-74). Morgantown, WV: Fitness Information Technology.

Nideffer, R. M., and Sagal, M. S. (2001). Concentration and attention control training. In J. M. Williams (Ed.), *Applied sport psychology: Personal growth to peak performance* (4th ed., pp. 312-332). Mountain View, CA: Mayfield.

Smoll, F. L. (2001). Coach-parent relationship in youth sport: Increasing harmony and minimizing hassle. In J.M. Williams (Ed.), *Applied sport psychology: Personal growth to peak performance* (4th ed., pp. 150-161). Mountain View, CA: Mayfield.

Tremayne, P., and Newbery, G. (2005). Mental skill training program for children. In D. Hackfort, J. L. Duda, and R. Lidor (Eds.), *Handbook of research in applied sport and exercise psychology: International perspectives* (pp. 93-108). Morgantown, WV: Fitness Information Technology.

Weiner, B. (1986). *An attribution theory of motivation and emotion.* NY: Springer-Verlag.

Weiss, M. (1991). Psychological skill development in children and adolescents. *The Sport Psychologist, 5,* 335-354.

Williams, J. M., and Harris, D. W. (2001). Relaxation and energizing techniques for regulation of arousal. In J. M. Williams (Ed.), *Applied sport psychology: Personal growth to peak performance* (4th ed., pp. 229-246). Mountain View, CA: Mayfield.

Zinsser, N., Bunker, L., and Williams, J. M. (2006). Cognitive techniques for building confidence and enhancing performance. In J. M. Williams (Ed.), *Applied sport psychology: Personal growth to peak performance* (5th ed., pp. 349-381). Boston: McGraw-Hill.

Chapter 6

PSYCHOLOGICAL SKILLS TRAINING FOR ATHLETES WITH DISABILITY AND SPORT INJURIES

ABSTRACT

Chapter 6 provides a short review of the existing literature in the area of psychological preparation for athletes with disability and sport injuries. The authors provide three case studies in which psychological skills training (PST) programs for judo, table tennis, and sailing 470 are described. These PST programs were applied for athletes' psychological preparation for the 2004 Olympic and Paralympic Games . The work with injured and disabled athletes requires some modifications to the ordinary psychological techniques. The modifications are applied based on the specific injury and the disability class. Much more research is needed to determine the appropriate format and context of these programs.

INTRODUCTION

Sport is an activity that places the mind and body under extreme stress, which can lead to injuries. While for most athletes' preparation for competition and competition itself are stressful, injury brings an added set of pressures (Brewer, 2010; Brewer and Tripp, 2005; Pargman, 2007). Therefore, athletes are required to be mentally tough in order to overcome injuries and achieve excellence while coping with physical disabilities. Eight out of every ten athletes will be injured at some time in their career, frequently while at college, and will miss at least three weeks of practice and competition in a season (Dulberg, 1988).

Research findings in the area of sport injuries and rehabilitation have indicated the following:

1. On one hand, there is a positive relationship between life stressors and injury (Williams and Anderson, 1998), and on the other hand there is a connection between injury and negative psychological states among athletes (Pargman, 2007).
2. Generalized muscle tension in training can lead to fatigue, as well as reduced flexibility and motor coordination, which increase the chances of high-risk injuries (Williams and Anderson, 1998).
3. There is a strong relationship between injuries and personality variables (factors) such as trait anxiety, locus of control, optimism-pessimism, aggression, gender, attentional style, and mood state (Williams, Rotella, and Scherzer, 2001).
4. Important factors in the recovery process are attitude, stress control, social support, goal setting, positive self-talk, mental imagery, and the belief of the individual regarding the effectiveness of the treatments he/she is undertaking (Ievleva and Orlick, 1991; Pargman, 2007).
5. The length of the rehabilitation process is shorter when athletes take control and feel accountable (Pargman, 2007).
6. Psychological interventions/strategies that have been examined experimentally in the context of sport injury rehabilitation include relaxation, biofeedback training, goal setting , imagery, and self-talk (Brewer and Tripp, 2005).

In the following three examples, we will try to demonstrate different aspects of our approach for improving the rehabilitation process after injury (judo), and also to describe PST programs for athletes with disabilities (table tennis and sailing – 470).

CASE 18: JUDO – FAST COMEBACK FROM THE REHABILITATION PROCESS TO THE OLYMPIC GAMES

This amazing story is about a young judoka, one year before the 2004 Olympic Games in Athens. The main goal of the judoka was to achieve the criteria to be part of the Olympic delegation. At that time the judoka worked with BB on a nonsystematic schedule, which meant having a consultation every once in a while. In September 2003 the judoka had a car accident, from which he suffered a serious abdominal injury. He had to undergo surgery, and he was not mobile for a period of a few weeks. At the end of September, when the judoka was allowed to walk, he arrived at BB's office. The judoka was very agitated, since he felt that his goals and dreams to compete at the Olympic Games had vanished. First of all, BB spoke with the doctors in order to understand the health status of the athlete. Only after the athlete received medical consent did BB continue the dialogue. He attempted to determine how much the judoka was determined to achieve his past goals. To help the judoka decide how committed he was, BB gave him examples of athletes who came back after serious injuries and were able to achieve excellence. Further, those athletes succeeded because of their mental toughness and obligation to the rehabilitation process.

Then BB asked the judoka how serious he was regarding his past goal to participate in the Olympic Games. The judoka said that this was his main goal, but now he had doubts regarding his ability to achieve it. BB worked with him on developing general (until the Olympic Games) and specific (a few months) plans for mapping the road to goal achievement. This process led the judoka to understand and believe that his goal could be realistic. The last important point was emphasizing the importance of psychological training as part of the rehabilitation process. That was not easy for the judoka, since before the injury he connected with BB only occasionally. The judoka agreed to obligate himself to the above terms.

The PST program for this athlete included short versions of RTP, SPTP, and the Wingate 5-Steps approach, all of which followed three phases: (1) *The learning* phase, in which the judoka practiced fundamental psychological techniques, such as relaxation, concentration, imagery, self-talk, biofeedback training, and reaction-training program (see Chapter 1 for more details); (2) The *modified* phase, in which the above techniques were adjusted to the athlete's situation and specific sport. For example, the imagery exercises lasted for 5 minutes, similar to the length of a judo match; fast concentration and relaxation was used in between judo matches; and a reaction training program performed with stress impact was provided (see Chapter 1); and (3) The *applied* phase, in which the judoka performed the techniques accompanied by stress factors such as noise, films, touching, and demands. As a consequence of this process, the techniques were integrated into the preperformance routine in practice and competition.

During the months of October and November, the judoka trained in the fitness hall with an athletic trainer only on hand and leg strength. In addition, he continued to work with medical and physical therapist staff as part of the rehabilitation process. However, his main work was with BB, meeting with him twice per week.

Follows are a few examples of BB's meeting with the Judoka:

Wednesday, October 1, 2003, Laboratory setting
Introduction Part:
- Discussion on the judoka's current medical and motivation state
- Goal setting for the week.

Main Part:
- Concentration exercise with Galvanic Skin Response Biofeedback (GSR BFB): 10 sec x 10 times
- Reaction Training Program: 15-30-30 x 3 times
- Relaxation for 3-5 minutes x 2 times
- Imagery: External perspective of the judoka's best match.

Final Part:
- Relaxation with music for 10 minutes.

During the month of December the judoka started to practice simple judo exercises with his coach, and continued physical fitness training with the athletic coach. In the psychological program, the work was in the modified phase. Below we present an example of one of the meetings:

Thursday, December 16, 2003, Laboratory setting
Introduction Part:

- Discussion of the current medical and psychological state; analysis of the technical aspects of the judoka's performance

Main part:

- Reaction Training Program (RTP) second level: 15-30-30 (Simple 165 ms; Choice 175 ms; Discrimination 165 ms)
- Concentration exercise: 10 sec x 10 times
- Imagery: 5 min x 2 times. Internal perspective, match against one of his main opponents. Special attention to the technical tactical aspects of his performance
- Relaxation: 1-3 min x 2 times.

Final part:

- Relaxation with music: 5 min; BFB games.

During the months of January-February, 2004 the judoka started practice matches in judo with partners, therefore we used in our meetings (applied phase) techniques to develop and improve his pre-competitive routine. Moreover, some of the techniques were applied in his training.

Tuesday, January 6, 2004, Laboratory setting
Introduction part:

- Concentration exercise: 10 sec. x 10 times
- Goal setting: Performance goals.

Main part:

- RTP third level with competition noise and film fragments: 15-30-30 (Simple 160 ms; Choice 170 ms; Discrimination 165 ms) x 3 times
- Imagery: 5 min x 2 times. Matches against one of his main opponents (Russia or Germany). Special attention to technical and tactical aspects of performance
- Relaxation: 1-3 min x 2 times.

Final part:

- Relaxation with music: 5 min; BFB games

In the evening BB visited the judo team's practice to observe the athlete's performance and assist in applying some of the mental techniques learned in the laboratory. For example, concentration before warm up, fast relaxation after warm up, imagery between matches, and relaxation after practice.

**Table 6.1. The Judoka's Achievements during the Years
2001-2004 in Significant Competitions**

	Tournament A	European Championship	Olympic Games
2000	Minck – I Lounding – 2		
2001	Sofia – 3		
2003	Tbilisi – 3	Dusseldorf – 5	
2004	Tbilisi – 1		1 win, 1 loss

During the months of March-April the athlete took part in various tournaments to achieve the criteria for the Olympic Games. The condition was to achieve first place in one of the tournaments (for his results, see Table 6.1). During this period there was a cooperative relationship between BB and the medical staff – the physician, therapist, and massagist – and with the athletic coach. Each of them provided the judoka with the professional and social support needed. The judoka took part willingly in his rehabilitation, since he was involved in the decision making process and felt strictly disciplined and personally responsible towards the training program, both physically and mentally.

The judoka's investment, together with the support of the highly professional team, led to the achievement of his main goal: a ticket and participation at the Olympic Games in Athens.

In the next two cases we will discuss psychological preparation for athletes with *disabilities* (see Hanrahan, 1995; Martin, 2010). Most of the studies in the area have focused on the descriptive profiles of athletes with disabilities, with the most heavily investigated domain being that of mood states (e.g., Henschen, Horvat, and Ruswal, 1992). The content of any PST program should be designed on the basis of the needs of the athletes involved; however, the techniques and skills are usually similar across athletes and sports (Martin, 2010).

CASE 19: TABLE TENNIS – LONG-TERM COOPERATION WITH A DISABLE ELITE ATHLETE

This case is about a table tennis athlete with disability, categorized in class 3, disability group of spinal cord injury and bracial plexus (left), from 1997. In

September 2005 the athlete contacted BB with a request to begin a long-term cooperation to achieve his dream to earn a place at the 2008 Paralympic Games. At that time the athlete was in about 49-50th place in the world rating. In the first few meetings BB and the athlete spoke about his achievements in the past several competitions, and they analyzed the athlete's behavior before and during the games. Based on the information he collected, BB proposed a PST program focusing on concentration and self-regulation skills, as well as muscle relaxation before and during the game, and he developed a competitive plan for optimal performance. An obstacle that BB faced was that due to his disability the athlete could not perform some of the traditional psychological techniques. Therefore, BB had to either modify or create new exercises that would suit the athlete's needs.

One of the psychological techniques that the athlete had to master was *muscle relaxation*. Since our athlete was disabled on one side of his body, BB had to modify and apply the muscle relaxation exercise only to the right hand. An exercise was developed in which instead of contracting and relaxing a muscle, the athlete was asked to raise his right shoulder and immediately let it go down, in order to achieve a feeling of relaxation. The athlete was asked to perform this exercise a few times a day during a long time period (2-3 months). Initially, the athlete did this exercise in the laboratory by himself and then in training. During training the exercise was used before games, between points, after mistakes, and in any other stressful situation. After the athlete felt comfortable with the exercise BB guided him to apply it in local competitions, and eventually during international games. The athlete reported that the exercise improved his readiness for games and his coping abilities during games, especially after mistakes and before critical points.

Another technique BB and the athlete worked on was *concentration* exercise. In this case there were no critical modifications to this technique, which was performed with GSR BFB. In this case the athlete concentrated on breathing, and through the GSR data his progress could be observed. The length of the concentration exercises was short, lasting 10-15-20 seconds, and they were repeated 10 times for each time length. During one meeting the athlete performed three sets. For example, 10 sec x 10 times, 3 sets.

In addition, the RTP was used to improve the athlete's concentration and decision making abilities. The RT program included three motor tasks: simple Reaction Time (RT), two choice RT, and discrimination RT. The simple (10 times) and the discrimination (20 times) tasks were performed by the athlete with no modifications. However, modifications had to be made to the two choices RT (20 times) in which athlete reacted only to the right-side stimuli while BB helped with reactions to the left stimuli.

To achieve progress in table tennis, the connection between *muscle relaxation* and *concentration* is critical. The athlete reported that often during games, when he achieved high concentration, his muscles were tense, which interrupted his technique. Therefore, BB developed a special exercise for this case – the "stop-reaction" exercise. In this motor task the athlete held a wide stop-watch while his thumb pressed on the start-stop button. The main goal of this exercise was to start and stop the time as fast as possible. To achieve good results the athlete must learn how to relax his muscle and concentrate on the act. In the first meeting, the athlete's results were 17-18 seconds. After mastering the basic technique of the exercise, BB developed a special program that imitated the reality of a tennis table game. BB asked the athlete to image a competition in which each stop-watch result of 16 seconds or faster gave him one point. When the reaction time was slower than 16 seconds, the athlete's opponent earned a point in the game. All games lasted until 11 points were made. After one month of training BB changed the athlete's goal, since his results were 13-14 seconds. Achieving results of 13-14 seconds gave the athlete a point. Ultimately, our athlete performed the exercise in 11 seconds. This exercise was used in many variations, where each time the athlete had to achieve different results based on his opponent's level. In one training session 5-6 "stop-reaction" exercises were provided. Some examples are in Table 6.2 below.

When the athlete performed the stop-reaction exercise he used relaxation, concentration, and self-talking techniques. As in real-life competition, the athlete could take breaks, drink water, and wipe his hands in order to be prepare for the next point. In addition, during this exercise BB used background noises of competition in order to enhance the athlete's performance. The overall goal was to simulate and anticipate upcoming games and different competition situations, and observe the athlete's corresponding behavior.

This special PST program helped the athlete to achieve and to improve his results from 2005 to 2011 (the present). In 2005 the athlete was ranked 49-50th in the world rating. In 2006 our plan was to achieve 30th place, and athlete achieved 23rd place. In 2007, to be part of the Paralympic delegation, the athlete had to be among the 30 best world players. He achieved 15th place. In the Paralympic games of 2008 he was rated among the top 10 table tennis players. Today, 2011, the athlete is among the first 10 players and stands at 9th place.

Throughout the psychological cooperation the athlete demonstrated strong character and a high level of motivation. The athlete admitted that a significant part of his achievements were due to the psychological skills he acquired. The same approach is presently being used with four other disabled athletes from table tennis who have demonstrated significant progress in their competition performance.

Table 6.2. Example of the Athlete's Results in the "Stop-Reaction" Exercise

Game 1: 12 sec or faster = 1 point		Game 2: 11 sec or faster = 1 point	
Athlete's Results	Game Score	Athlete's Results	Game Score
12	1:0	12	0:1
11	2:0	11	1:1
12	3:0	12	1:2
11	4:0	13	1:3
16	4:1	11	2:3
11	5:1	12	2:4
14	5:2	11	3:4
12	6:2	12	3:5
15	6:3	10	4:5
12	7:3	12	4:6
9	8:4	14	4:7
11	9:4	11	5:7
12	10:4	11	6:7
13	10:5	11	7:8
11	11:5	11	8:8
		11	9:8
		11	10:8
		9	11:8

CASE 20: SAILING 470 –
FROM LABORATORY TO BOAT

In 2003 the coach of a sailing team who competed on the sonar three-person keelboat approached BB for psychological support. His team, made up of disabled athletes (two athletes with amputations and one athlete with spinal injury), was training for the 2004 Athens Paralympic Games. That was the first Olympic experience for both the coach and the athletes. During a meeting with BB the coach analyzed previous competitions, in which he observed many mistakes. He stressed the impact of wrong decision making in simple situations and problematic relationship between athletes as affecting the athletes' performance. BB visited the marina, met and talked with the athletes, and joined the athletes (by to their invitation) on sea training on the coach boat and later on the athlete's boat. During the first month BB took part in their sea training. This experience helped BB understand the hierarchy between the athletes and the coach. In addition, it was important to comprehend the overall demands of athletes with disabilities in this sport. Beyond that, BB collected information on the athletes' communication, leadership, decision making, and stress management.

After the first month BB met with the athletes after training, to explain his impressions and recommendations, which were based on his experience at three Olympic Games (1992, 1996, 2000). An important issue that was raised was the overall attitude of the athletes to the training process. The athletes did not keep to a structured training regime, and their behavior before and during practice was not professional. The athletes spent their time on discussions and arguments instead of on decision making and performance. This had an effect on the athletes' relationship with each other and on their obligation to achievement. Based on that, BB, with full cooperation from the coach, recommended some important principles, such as "one team – one family" and "one team – one goal". That led to an absolute commitment to the team goal – achieving a medal in the Paralymic Games. The implications of this were observed during training: The athletes worked around a demanding schedule and invested all they had in each training ("when I train – I really train"). This simple principle upon which the athletes agreed had a drastic effect on the overall training atmosphere. The athletes began to come early to training in order to prepare themselves and the boat for maximum effectiveness during

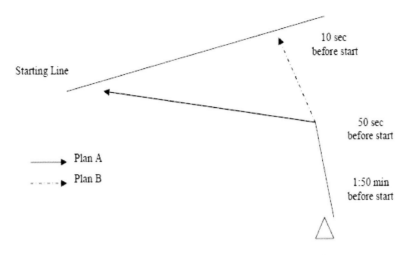

Figure 6.1. Example of a starting race: Basic plan A and a reserve plan B.

practice. This behavior had a positive effect on the concentration level during practice, cooperation with the athletes before training, and their overall readiness.

The next step of psychological support with the sailing team was to understand the challenges the athletes faced during the race. Therefore, BB asked each athlete to give him a road map of a competition race. Each athlete drew and analyzed it separately. The road map included the competition path from start to finish, with specific, somewhat problematic points. For example, during the starting point the athletes had to work on their decision-making process regarding which strategy plan they should choose, along with their corresponding behavior. Another example was a curve in the path in which the sailors had to decide in which style they had to "attack" the mark (i.e., float) while considering other boats.

As can be seen in Figure 6.1, all sonar boats start from the starting line. The sailors follow the path and have to pass floats until they arrive at the finish line.

All three athletes and the coach marked the starting spot as an important and problematic point. A good start can determine the quality and the performance level of the race. On the other hand, a bad start can be an additional obstacle and a stress factor to deal with during the race. Therefore, BB helped the team to develop an optimal pre-start routine in order to establish a controlled and effective mental state. This helped the team to focus on the important acts to be performed before and during a race. Basic plan A and a reserve plan B were developed (see Figure 6.1). The sailors practiced the plans through imagery. First the practice took part on the beach and later in the boat. The three sailors practiced the starting scene together while BB verbally marked three important time points: 1:50 min, 50 sec, and 10 sec before the start. During that time the team verbally practiced the commands and actions they had to perform during a real race. They practiced this scene 4-5 times during each meeting, for one month. Then the team practiced this imagery exercise on the boat, and finally applied the plan during competitions.

The goal of plan B was to give the athletes an additional option in case problems arose during Plan A. Plan B was shorter than plan A and started from the 50 sec marked point. The difference in time gave the athletes the opportunity to identify a problem and to allow them enough time for change and modification. The skipper was the only one who could make the decision whether or not plan A should be replaced.

In addition to team work, one-on-one consultation meetings were provided. The goal was to improve the concentration and self-regulation skills of the individual sailors. The psychological techniques included concentration exercises with GSR BFB, muscle relaxation, self-talking, BFB training, goal-setting and positive thinking. The sailing team achieved its goal and earned a gold medal in the 2004 Athens Paralympic Games.

CONCLUSION

This chapter focused on psychological support for athletes who have to deal with injuries and disabilities. First, BB felt it was an honor to work with the above athletes. To be a competitive athlete is a challenging task – more so when you need to deal with injury or disability. Therefore, psychological support is strongly recommended for this population. Psychological consultation is necessary for injured athletes for a fast comeback to training, while disabled athlete need the psychological support to achieve potential. Today the Paralympics is a significant sport event. For example, in Athens (2004) 4,000 athletes from 130 counties took part in this event, while only 400 athletes from 23 counties competed in the Rome Paralympics (1960) (International Council of Sport Science and Physical Education Bulletin, 2004). And lastly, working with injured and disabled athletes requires some modifications to the psychological techniques. These modifications are applied based on the injury and the class of disability. As was mentioned in the beginning of the summary, it is an honor to work with disabled athletes. These athletes strongly appreciate and positively evaluate the sport psychology support.

REFERENCES

Brewer, B. W. (2010). Adherence to sport injury rehabilitation. In S. Hanrahan and M. Andersen (Eds.), *Routledge handbook of applied sport psychology: A comprehensive guide for students and practitioners* (pp. 233-241). London and New York: Routledge, Taylor and Francis Group.

Brewer, B. W., and Tripp, D. A.(2005). Psychological applications in the prevention and rehabilitation of sport injuries. In D. Hackfort, J. Duda, and R. Lidor (Eds.), *Handbook of research in applied sport and exercise psychology: International perspectives* (pp. 319-334). Morgantown, WV: Fitness Information Technology.

Dulberg, H. N. (1988). Injury: How athletes deal with hurt. *Sport Care and Fitness, 2,* 53.

Hanrahan, S. (1995). Sport psychology for athletes with disabilities. In T. Morris and J. Summers (Eds.), *Sport psychology: Theory, application and issues* (pp. 502-515). Milton, Qld: John Wiley and Sons.

Henschen, K. L., Horvat, M., and Roswal, G. (1992). Psychological profiles of the United States wheelchair basketball team. *International Journal of Sport Psychology, 23*(2), 128-137.

Ievleva, L., and Orlick, T. (1991). Mental links to enhance healing: An exploratory study. *The Sport Psychologist, 5,* 25-40.

International Council of Sport Science and Physical Education (ICSSPE) Bulletin (2004). Paralympic games participation statistics, 41, 1-2. http://www.icsspe.org/bulletin/bulletin.php?v=246andkat=5andNo=41andl =2andpar=1.

Martin, J. J (2010). Athletes with physical disabilities. In S. Hanrahan and M. Andersen (Eds.), *Routledge handbook of applied sport psychology: A comprehensive guide for students and practitioners* (pp. 432-440). London and New York: Routledge, Taylor and Francis Group.

Pargman, D. (2007). Sport injury: A psychological perspective. In B. Blumenstein, R. Lidor, and G. Tenenbaum (Eds.), *Psychology of sport training* (pp. 186-215). Oxford, UK: Meyer and Meyer Sport.

Williams, J. M., and Andersen, M. B. (1998). Psychosocial antecedents of sport injury: Review and critique of the stress and injury model. *Journal of Applied Sport Psychology, 10*, 5-25.

Williams, J., Rottenly, R., and Scherzer, C. (2001). Injury risk and rehabilitation: Psychological consideration. In J. Williams (Ed.), *Applied sport psychology: Personal growth to peak performance* (4th ed., pp. 456-479). Mountain View, CA: Mayfield.

Chapter 7

Lessons Learned from Mental Practice in Sport

Abstract

The field of psychological skills training (PST) has developed rapidly over the last two decades. The message of this book is clear: the aim of the applied sport psychology consultant should be to create a psychological skills training program that would enable the athlete to cope with competitive stress. Seven main points for developing PST programs are presented in chapter 7: (1) PST as part of overall athlete's preparation; (2) PST should be based on periodization principle; (3) PST can be provided in various framework; (4) For PST to be successful full cooperation with coach and athlete is needed; (5) The cooperation between consultant and other sport professional is important; (6) Answers the demand for successful consulting in sport; and (7) PST must be based on research.

Introduction

Psychological Skills Training (PST) is a relatively new field of research and practice, still in the process of development. Numerous researchers have indicated that successful athletes and coaches may use PST as multimodal interventions which combine several mental training techniques (e.g., Vealey, 2007). On the other hand, athletes may use mental practice techniques such as imagery, relaxation, self-talking, biofeedback (BFB) training, and goal setting individually (Gould, 2006; Morris, Spittle, and Watt, 2005; Williams, 2006).

Overall, PST has been found to be effective in improving athletes' performance both in individual and team sports. At the same time, the integration of PST as part of the training program is not yet completely established. However, athletes and coaches report on using mental techniques relatively frequently during competitions (Frey, Laguna, and Ravizza, 2003)

SEVEN POINTS FOR DEVELOPING PSYCHOLOGICAL SKILLS TRAINING

The effectiveness of PST has been strongly established based on experience and research, which leads to the question "Why is PST not an integral part of the modern training process?". In the following points we discuss important conclusions and guidelines to be considered in order to effectively include PST as part of the training process.

First Point: PST as Part of the Athlete's Overall Preparation

PST is only one aspect of an athlete's preparation. The literature on theory and methodology of sport training maintains that athletic preparation is composed of physical, technical, tactical, and psychological preparations (Bompa, 1999; Carrera and Bompa, 2007). Therefore, each athlete's preparation must include a full integration of the psychological aspect in order to accomplish maximum achievement. There is some support from research and applied work for the inclusion of PST as part of the training process (see Balague, 2000; Blumenstein, Lidor, and Tenenbaum, 2007; Blumenstein and Weinstein, 2010). All 20 case studies which were presented in this book strengthen this concept.

Second Point: Mental Practice and the Periodization Principle

The periodization principle is a fundamental concept in the theory and methodology of sport training, already published in the former USSR during the 1950s, and more recently in Western countries (Bompa, 1984). However, only in the beginning of the 21st century have researchers and practitioners in sport psychology discussed the importance of the principle when designing

PST programs (Balague, 2000; Blumenstein et al., 2007; Blumenstein and Weinstein, 2010; Holliday et al., 2008). In the first chapter the periodization principle as applied to sport and PST was discussed.

The realization of the periodization principle when designing PST programs should be applied in two directions. First, it is important to choose the psychological strategies according to the training period (preparation, competition, transition). For example, during the *preparation phase*, especially during general preparation, the athlete should improve his/her working capacity, namely to help the athlete to adapt to the physical and psychological demands of the training program. The athlete's training is characterized by a high volume of monotonous physical work that is made up of a large number of exercises and repetitions. In this period psychological support, such as strengthening motivation, goal setting, and psychological recovery, can help the athlete cope with training stress. In the *competition phase* the intensity of technical elements increases and the repetitions decrease; therefore, the appropriate psychological elements will focus more on concentration, short relaxation exercises, pre-competitive routines, etc. (see Blumenstein et al., 2007). In the *transition phase* psychological support focuses more on relaxation and goal setting strategies, in preparation for the upcoming sports season.

Second, the psychological strategies should be modified along the training process. Most of the psychological techniques go through three phases: (1) learning, in which the athlete learns basic fundamental psychological techniques in a laboratory setting; (2) modification, in which the athlete trains and modifies techniques and strategies according to the sport's demands (duration, intensity, sport-specificity). This phase is usually provided in laboratory and training settings; and (3) application, in which the athlete applies the techniques as part of a precompetitive or pre-performance routine.

Third Point: PST's Frameworks

PST has a positive effect on athletic performance. In our work we use different PST programs, such as systematic, non-systematic, situational, and educational programs. The systematic PST is based on a long-term relationship with the sport psychology consultant, reflected a program of 1-2 meetings per week, in laboratory, training, and competition settings (see Cases 1, 3, 6, and 11). The non-systematic PST program is provided with voluntary pauses; such as working with the athlete for a specific period, goal, or competition (see Cases 2 and 17). The situational PST program is related to a concrete situation towards which the athletes or team is working. The main goal of the psychological consultation is to prepare the athlete to achieve in that specific situation (see Cases 10 and 16). We often observed that when the athlete finalized his/her mental training there was no significant progress in future competitive performance. In some cases, after an unsuccessful performance the athletes dropped out of sport.

Lastly, educational PST includes lectures and workshops on psychological topics during conferences and professional meetings, to improve athlete-coach knowledge.

Fourth Point: Full Cooperation with Coach and Athlete

The relationship between the sport psychology consultant and the athlete/coach is critical for the integration of PST into the training process. For full cooperation to be established, the coach must be aware of the concepts and procedures of the PST process. However, we found in our research that psychological awareness and knowledge regarding PST is relatively weak among professional coaches (Blumenstein and Orbach, 2010). This conflict can have a significantly negative impact on the relationship between the consultant-coach-athlete. The coach knows the importance of psychological preparation for competition, but since he/she may not have enough knowledge about PST, he/she sometimes prefers to neglect it.

Blumenstein and Weinstein (2010) suggested four cooperation scenarios between the coach-athlete-consultant. The scenarios were based on the agreement or disagreement of the coach (C) and the athlete (A) in regard to the use of PST. For example, an optimal relationship can be observed when the coach and the athlete both are aware of and agree to PST (C+ A+). In this scenario the cooperation develops according to the steps presented in Figure 7.1.

There are three more possible scenarios which describe the relationship between the consultant and athlete/coach: C- A+ (coach does not believe in the importance of PST while the athlete does); C+ A- (coach does believe in the importance of PST while the athlete does not); C- A- (both do not believe in the importance of PST). Based on the scenario, the consultant should decide which intervention and approach is the most appropriate for that situation.

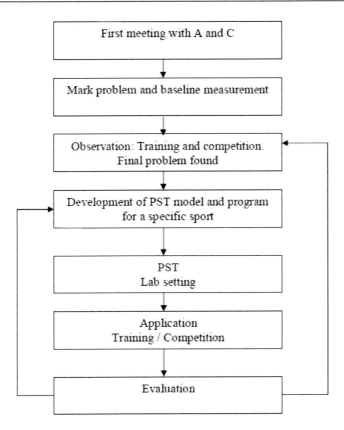

Figure 7.1. Steps of Cooperation: Scenario C+ A+.

Fifth Point: Cooperation between Consultant and Sport Professionals

The success of the sport psychology consultant support relates to the relationship among and cooperation with different sport professionals, such as the nutritionist, masseur/masseuse, athletic trainer, officials, physician, and finally the athlete's friends and family. To optimize these relationships the sport psychology consultant provides various educational materials through lectures, conferences, workshops, discussions, one-time consultations, e-mails, phone calls, articles, etc. The influence of the above individuals can have an important effect on the athlete, and can change the athlete's/coach's mood, motivation, and self-confidence.

Sixth Point: Demands for Successful Consulting in Sport

Who is the sport psychology consultant? It is essential for the consultant to have an understanding regarding his/her role and function in the training process. There are cases in which the consultant provides the athlete with psychological "first aid", and other times the relationships are based on long-term support and psychological training.

Being empathetic, patient, communicative, a good listener, and attentive are necessary foundations for successful sport psychology consulting (Murphy and Murphy, 2010). In addition, the consultant should be ready to adapt to a flexible schedule in which he/she may need to attend events in various locations and cope with different kinds of competition stress. The above requirements can be fulfilled by a person who loves and understands various sport disciplines.

Seventh Point: PST Must be Based on Research

Successful performance by the athlete/team is usually related or attributed to good psychological preparation. However, we need to develop norms and hard data to arrive at conclusions regarding the effectiveness of PST in different sports. In our case studies, we tended to use many psychophysiological measures, such as Heart Rate (HR), Galvanic Skin Response (GSR), and Electromyography (EMG), to keep the information objective. Psychological cognitive strategies such as BFB training and reaction-training programs were used in our case studies. Based on the data, we developed norms and levels for various sports.

The methods we used and described in this book are only some of the many approaches that are being used in sport psychology (see Vealey, 2007). We believe in the effectiveness of our PST program, which may be linked with cultural differences, sport history, and experience. We would like to end this book with a short anecdote: In 1990, when BB started to work with local athletes in Israel, he "made a deal" with his clients. Each athlete who achieved a medal from European, World Championships, or Olympic Games had to give a picture to BB to put on his office wall. The athletes often laughed and commented that the wall would stay empty up until BB's retirement. Today, BB is still working, however he has no more space for additional pictures on his office walls!

Therefore, we want to thank all the coaches and athletes with whom we have worked, and we would like to emphasize a very simple rule: "When You Believe, It Is Possible". We hope that this book demonstrates the main road to success.

REFERENCES

Balague, G. (2000). Periodization of psychological skills training. *Journal of Science and Medicine in Sport*, 3, 230-237.

Blumenstein, B., and Weinstein,Y. (2010). *Psychological skills training: Application to elite sport performance*. Grand Rapids, MI: Ultimate Athlete Concepts.

Blumenstein, B., Lidor, R., and Tenenbaum, G. (2007) (Eds.). *Psychology of sport training*. Oxford, UK: Meyer and Meyer Sport.

Blumenstein, B., and Orbach, I. (2010). The profile of the professional coach. *Applied Research in Coaching and Athletics Annual, 25*, 213-231.

Bompa, T. (1984). *Theory and methodology of training – The key to athletic performance*. Boca Raton, FL: Kendall/Hunt.

Bompa, T. (1999). *Periodization: Theory and methodology of training* (4th ed.). Champaign, IL: Human Kinetics.

Carrera, M., and Bompa, T. (2007). Theory and methodology of training: General perspectives. In B. Blumenstein, R. Lidor, and G. Tenenbaum (Eds.), *Psychology of sport training* (pp. 19-39). Oxford, UK: Meyer and Meyer Sport.

Frey, M., Laguna, P. L., and Ravizza, K. (2003). Collegiate athletes' mental skill use and perceptions of success: An exploration of the practice and competition settings. *Journal of Applied Sport Psychology, 15*, 115-128.

Gould, D. (2006). Goal setting for peak performance. In J. M. Williams (Ed.), *Applied sport psychology: Personal growth to peak performance* (5th ed., pp. 240-259). Boston: McGraw-Hill.

Holliday, B., Burton, D., Sun, G., Hammermeister, J., Naylor, S., and Freigang, D. (2008). Building the better mental training mousetrap: Is periodization a more systematic approach to promoting performance excellence? *Journal of Applied Sport Psychology, 20*, 199-219.

Morris, T., Spittle, M., and Watt, A. P. (2005) *Imagery in sport*. Champaign, IL: Human Kinetics.

Murphy, S., and Murphy, A. (2010) Attending and listening. In S. Hanrahan and M. Andersen (Eds.), *Routledge Handbook of Applied Sport*

Psychology: A comprehensive guide for students and practitioners (pp.12-20). London and New York: Routledge, Taylor and Francis Group.

Vealey, R. (2007). Mental skills training in sport. In G. Tenenbaum, and R. Eklund (Eds.), *Handbook of sport psychology* (3rd ed., pp. 287-309). New York: Wiley.

Williams, J. M. (Ed.) (2006). *Applied sport psychology: Personal growth to peak performance* (5th ed.). Boston: McGraw-Hill.

ABOUT THE AUTHORS

Dr. Boris Blumenstein is the Director of the Department of Behavioral Sciences at the Ribstein Center for Sport Medicine Sciences and Research, Wingate Institute, Israel. He received his Ph.D. in Sport Psychology in 1980 from the All Union Institute for Research in Sport, Department of Sport Psychology, Moscow, Russia (former USSR). His extensive experience in sport psychology spans some 30 years, culminating in applied work at the elite level. He was a sport psychology consultant for the Soviet national and Olympic teams and, since 1990 to the Israeli national and Olympic teams (including the delegations to the Atlanta 1996, Sydney 2000, Athens 2004, and Beijing 2008 Olympics). He is author and coauthor of over 90 refereed journal articles and book chapters, mainly in the area of sport and exercise psychology. Dr. Blumenstein is the senior editor of the book "Brain and Body in Sport and Exercise: Biofeedback Applications in Performance Enhancement", published by Wiley (2002), "Psychology of Sport Training", published by Meyer and Meyer Sport (2007), and "Psychological Skills Training: Application to Elite Sport Performance, published by Ultimate Athlete Concepts (2010). He has also given more than 80 scientific presentations at international and national conferences and workshops. His current research interests include mental skills training for enhanced performance, stress-performance relationships, the effectiveness of different mental interventions, and athletic competition readiness. In addition, he is a past president of the Israeli Society for Sport Psychology.

Dr. Iris Orbach is a researcher and a sport psychology consultant in the Department of Behavioral Sciences at the Ribstein Center for Sport Medicine Sciences and Research, Wingate Institute, Israel. She received her Ph.D. in Sport Psychology in 1999 from the University of Florida, Department of Sport and Exercise Sciences, in Gainesville, Florida, USA. She worked as an assistant professor for eight years in the Department of Sport, Fitness and Leisure Studies at Salem State University, Salem, Massachusetts, USA. In addition to teaching, Dr. Orbach has published numerous articles and book chapters, and has given presentations at national and international conferences on topics related to sport psychology. Her current research interests include stress-performance relationships, children and motivation in sport, and the effectiveness of various practices of mental training. Dr. Orbach uses her psychology skills as a consultant for athletes at all skill levels. In her free time, Dr. Orbach enjoys running, bicycling, swimming, weight lifting, and all kind of fitness activities.

ACKNOWLEDGMENTS

Most of the research for this book was conducted during our work at the Ribstein Center for Sport Medicine Sciences and Research, at the Elite Sport Department, and in the Sport Academy, all at the Wingate Institute. We would like to thank the athletes and coaches with whom we have worked in numerous international competitions, including four Olympic Games.

We are very grateful to our colleagues and friends, especially Professors Michael Bar-Eli, Ronnie Lidor, and Gershon Tenenbaum. A special thank you to Ms. Dinah Olswang who worked diligently on the technical and editorial side of the book.

We are also grateful to the fine editorial staff at Nova Publisher for their contribution and skill.

Finally, we wish to thank our families for their sincere and enthusiastic support of our work at all times.

INDEX

R

S